Cedar Rapids Convention Complex Parkade

Cedar Rapids, Iowa

FEMA 1763- DR-IA

May 16, 2012

FEMA

Federal Emergency Management Agency
Department of Homeland Security
9221 Ward Parkway, Suite 300
Kansas City, MO 64114

TABLE OF CONTENTS

TABLES

APPENDICES

Abbreviations and Acronyms

ACM	Asbestos Containing Material
APE	Area of Potential Effect
BMP	Best Management Practices
CAA	Clean Air Act
CEQ	Council on Environmental Quality
CFR	Code of Federal Regulations
CERCLA	Comprehensive Environmental Response, Compensation and Liability Act
CRCC	Cedar Rapids Convention Complex
dB	Decibels
EA	Environmental Assessment
EHP	Environmental Planning and Historic Preservation
EIS	Environmental Impact Statement

Abbreviations and Acronyms continued

EO	Executive Order
EPA	Environmental Protection Agency
ESA	Endangered Species Act
ESA	Environmental Site Assessment
FEMA	Federal Emergency Management Agency
FIRM	Flood Insurance Rate Map
FONSI	Finding of No Significant Impact
FPPA	Farmland Protection Policy Act
GHG	Greenhouse Gases
HMGP	Hazard Mitigation Grant Program
HPC	Historic Preservation Commission
HUD	U.S. Department of Housing and Urban Development
IHSEMD	Iowa Homeland Security and Emergency Management Division
IDNR	Iowa Department of Natural Resources
LUST	Leaking Underground Storage Tank
MPO	Metropolitan Planning Organization
NAAQS	National Ambient Air Quality Standards
NEPA	National Environmental Policy Act
NESHAP	National Emission Standards for Hazardous Air Pollutants
NFIP	National Flood Insurance Program
NHPA	National Historic Preservation Act
NPDES	National Pollutant Discharge Elimination System
NRCS	Natural Resources Conservation Service
NRHP	National Register of Historic Places
OSA	Office of the State Archaeologist
REC	Recognized Environmental Condition
RCRA	Resource Conservation and Recovery Act
RIO	Rebuild Iowa Office
SAFETEA-LU	Safe, Accountable, Flexible, Efficient Transportation Equity Act: A Legacy for Users
sf	Square Feet
SHPO	State Historic Preservation Office
SHSI	State Historic Society of Iowa
SWPPP	Storm Water Pollution Prevention Plan
USACE	U.S. Army Corps of Engineers
USDA	U.S. Department of Agriculture
UST	Underground Storage Tank
USFWS	U.S. Fish and Wildlife Service

1. INTRODUCTION

On May 27, 2008, President Bush declared a major disaster in the State of Iowa (1763-DR-IA) pursuant to the Robert T. Stafford Disaster Relief and Emergency Assistance Act, as amended, 42 U.S.C. Section 5121-5206. The incident period began on May 25, 2008 and closed August 13, 2008.

The National Environmental Policy Act (NEPA) requires that Federal agencies evaluate the environmental effects of their proposed and alternative actions before deciding to fund an action. The President's Council on Environmental Quality (CEQ) has developed a series of regulations for implementing the NEPA. These regulations are included in Title 40 of the Code of Federal Regulations (CFR), Parts 1500–1508. They require the preparation of an Environmental Assessment (EA) that includes an evaluation of alternative means of addressing the problem and a discussion of the potential environmental impacts of a proposed Federal action. An EA provides the evidence and analysis to determine whether the proposed Federal action will have a significant adverse effect on human health and the environment. An EA, as it relates to the FEMA program, must be prepared according to the requirements of the Stafford Act and 44 CFR, Part 10. This section of the Federal Code requires that FEMA take environmental considerations into account when authorizing funding or approving actions. This EA was conducted in accordance with both CEQ and FEMA regulations for NEPA and will address the environmental issues associated with the FEMA grant funding as applied to the construction of the Cedar Rapids Convention Complex Parkade (hereon "Parkade").

Executive Order (EO) 11988 (Floodplain Management) requires that Federal agencies assume a leadership role in avoiding direct or indirect support of development within the 100-year floodplain whenever there is a practicable alternative. Further, EO 11988 requires consideration of the 500-year floodplain for critical facilities such as hospitals and fire stations.

The City of Cedar Rapids is in the process of planning for and designing a new multi-story parking ramp on Lots 24/26 across 1st Avenue E from the Cedar Rapids Convention Complex (CRCC) and Hotel. This facility will be referred to as the Cedar Rapids Convention Complex Parkade. The Parkade will ultimately be connected to the new CRCC and Hotel via a skywalk over 1st Avenue E. The structure is intended to accommodate ground level retail units. The Parkade is being designed as a post-tensioned poured in place concrete structure with drilled piers. A contemporary façade would be used to compliment adjacent contemporary architecture and contrast with existing historic buildings. Lot 44 would be repaired to pre-disaster condition and therefore will not be considered in this EA. Cedar Rapids plans to have the new Parkade completed when the hotel and the adjacent CRCC, both closed for renovation, reopen in the fall of 2012. The new convention center next door is slated to open in early 2013.

A public notice will be published in the Cedar Rapids Gazette before or at the beginning of the 30-day public comment period; such a notice will also be available through the City's CR Progress webpage and FEMA Region VII's Environmental Documents and Public Notices webpage. Copies of this EA will be available for the duration of the public comment period at City Hall, Cedar Rapids Public Library at 221 3rd Street SE downtown and 2600 Edgewood Road SW at Westdale Mall, and on FEMA Environmental Documents and Public Notices website.

2. PURPOSE AND NEED

Pursuant to Section 406 of the Robert T. Stafford Disaster Relief and Emergency Assistance Act of 1974 (42 U.S.C. 5172), as amended, the City of Cedar Rapids has requested funding through FEMA Public Assistance Program. FEMA's Public Assistance Program provides supplemental Federal disaster grant assistance to State, Tribal, and local governments, and certain types of Private Nonprofit organizations so that communities can respond to and recover from major disasters or emergencies. The Public Assistance Program also has rules whereby eligible applicants may choose to use eligible, though capped, recovery funds for alternate or improved projects that may be more beneficial to the Applicant than what existed prior to the disaster event.

The purpose of this project is to improve parking capacity of Lots 24/26 in downtown Cedar Rapids by using the FEMA Public Assistance Program to contribute eligible funding toward improving the parking capacity of Lot 24/26. The Parkade will ultimately be connected to the new CRCC and Hotel via a skywalk over 1st Avenue E. The structure is intended to accommodate ground level retail units in downtown Cedar Rapids. The proposed site for the Parkade is currently Lots 24/26 parking facility and intersecting alley located between 1st Avenue E and 3rd Street SE; see Appendix A, Figure 1 and Appendix C, Figure 1.

The need for the proposed project is to increase the parking capacity of downtown Cedar Rapids. This project will provide adequate parking for the CRCC and Hotel that is currently under construction. This EA is intended to document the City's decision-making process and evaluate City and FEMA defined alternatives for the City's desire to improve the parking capacity of Lots 24/26.

The City of Cedar Rapids estimated cost of the ramp at $10.5 million and the skywalk at $1 million. In addition to the base design for the ramp and skywalk, the city developed four alternate bids for additions to the base project. The first add-on would provide a more-attractive exterior cladding on the side of the ramp that faces 2nd Avenue SE, which matches the basic bid for the two sides visible to 1st Avenue E. The fourth side, next to the Iowa Theatre Building home to Theatre Cedar Rapids would not be visible as it would abut the Iowa Theatre Building. The second add-on would add a seventh floor to the ramp. The basic bid calls for a multi-level structure with 460 parking spaces; potential to add another level with 75 parking spaces. The third add-on would provide for more first-floor retail space on the side of the ramp facing 1st Avenue SE than is called for in the basic bid. The fourth add-on would provide a faster elevator.

This EA is intended to document and evaluate Cedar Rapids and FEMA defined alternatives for the City's desire to use eligible recovery funds from the facilities considered here toward the construction of the Parkade under FEMA's improved project policies.

3. ALTERNATIVES ANALYSIS

NEPA requires the investigation and evaluation of reasonable project alternatives as part of the environmental review process for the proposed project. EO 11988 requires the investigation of practicable alternatives prior to Federal agencies taking actions that provide direct or indirect support of floodplain development. Inclusion of a No Action Alternative in the environmental analysis and documentation is required under NEPA. The No Action Alternative is used to evaluate the effects of not providing eligible assistance for the project, thus providing a benchmark against which "action alternatives" may be evaluated.

3.1 ALTERNATIVE 1 - NO ACTION

The No Action Alternative is defined as maintaining the status quo with no additional FEMA funding being provided for repairs. No repairs, code upgrades, or mitigation measures would be implemented. FEMA funding would be limited to the already completed cleanup and debris left by the flooding event and the functions of Lots 24/26 would continue to operate as a surface parking facility.

3.2 ALTERNATIVE 2 - PROPOSED ACTION

The Proposed Action is a FEMA improved project to construct the Parkade located on Lots 24/26 and the intersecting alley across 1st Avenue E from the CRCC. The Parkade will ultimately be connected to the new CRCC and Hotel via a skywalk over 1st Avenue E. The structure is intended to accommodate ground level retail units. The Parkade is being designed as a post-tensioned poured in place concrete structure with 42 drilled piers at a depth of 50 feet. Excavation would be limited to the removal of the existing pavement and potential spoil from non-extant building foundations. The footprint of the excavation would extend approximately 3 feet past the property line on 4th Street. A contemporary façade would be used to compliment adjacent contemporary architecture and contrast with existing historic buildings. Work on Lot 44 will be repaired to pre-disaster condition. Cedar Rapids plans to have the Parkade completed when the CRCC and Hotel, both closed for renovation, reopen in the fall of 2012. The new convention center next door is slated to open in early 2013.

Funding for this improved project is a combination of local option sales tax from the City of Cedar Rapids Local Option Sales Tax (LOST) and FEMA funding from the repair estimate for the existing Lots 24/26 and intersecting alley. Cedar Rapids is also applying eligible FEMA funding for the repair and/or replacement of 280 parkway sites throughout downtown Cedar Rapids including parkways, washouts, decorative benches, planters, decorative trash receptacles, granite surface washouts, monument tree and guard rails.

3.3 OTHER ALTERNATIVES CONSIDERED

Cedar Rapids has elected an improved project with alternate funding to build the Parkade. Because of this decision, FEMA is dismissing the alternative for the repair the existing Lots 24/26 facility and repair and/or replacement of 280 parkway sites throughout downtown Cedar Rapids including parkways, washouts, decorative benches, planters, decorative trash receptacles, granite surface washouts, monument tree and guard rails to pre-disaster condition with the inclusion of code upgrades and hazard mitigation measures. Cedar Rapids has informed FEMA that these 280 sites have been rendered safe and secure and therefore are not considered in this EA.

4. SUMMARY OF IMPACTS AND MITIGATION

No Action and the Proposed Action were evaluated in this EA and their impacts summarized in this section using the following scale. Impacts are assumed to be negative unless noted otherwise. The following section, Section 5, further details the anticipated impacts of both alternatives.

- No impact – no impacts are anticipated
- Negligible impact – no discernible impacts are anticipated or are minimal and cannot be measured meaningfully
- Minor impact – anticipated impacts are measurable, but are minor and within or below regulatory standards and/or are confined to the project site(s)
- Moderate impact – anticipated impacts are measurable and/or have impacts that may extend beyond the project site(s), may require permitting, and may require limited mitigation actions or coordination to minimize negative impacts
- Major impact – anticipated impacts are readily measurable, have a regional impact, require mitigation to reduce impacts, and/or exceed existing regulatory standards; permanent changes to the resources would be expected

Table 4-1: Summary of Impacts and Mitigation

Affected Environment	Impacts	Mitigation Measures / BMPs
Geology and Soils		
Alternative 1	No impact	Not applicable
Alternative 2	Minor to Moderate impact	Construction best management practices (BMP) are required to control soil erosion and sedimentation are required
Air Quality		
Alternative 1	Negligible to Minor impact	Not applicable
Alternative 2	Minor to Moderate impact (short term), Minor impact (long term)	BMP appropriate to site conditions and fugitive dust controls required to reduce short term impacts to minor to negligible levels
Climate Change		
Alternative 1	No impact	Not applicable
Alternative 2	No to Negligible impact	Not applicable
Water Quality		
Alternative 1	No to Negligible impact	Not applicable
Alternative 2	No to Minor impact	For ground disturbance of one acre or more, a Storm Water Pollution Prevention Plan and NPDES permit are required

Wetlands			
	Alternative 1	No to Negligible impact	Not applicable
	Alternative 2	No to Negligible impact	Appropriate sediment and erosion control BMP for ground-disturbing activities
Floodplain			
	Alternative 1	No to Negligible impact	Not applicable
	Alternative 2	No impact	Not applicable
Protected Species and Habitat			
	Alternative 1	No impact	Not applicable
	Alternative 2	No impact	Not applicable
Historic Structures			
	Alternative 1	No impact	Not applicable
	Alternative 2	Minor to moderate impact	FEMA consultation with State Historic Preservation Office (SHPO) may result in additional process to resolve adverse effects through Memorandum of Agreement (MOA)
Archaeology			
	Alternative 1	No to Negligible impact	Not applicable
	Alternative 2	Minor to major impact	FEMA consultation with State Historic Preservation Office (SHPO) may result in additional process to document potential archaeological deposits which if eligible for listing in the National Registry of Historic Places would result in MOA and constitute a major impact
Environmental Justice			
	Alternative 1	No to Negligible impact	Not applicable
	Alternative 2	Minor (positive) impact	Not applicable
Noise			
	Alternative 1	No to Negligible impact	Not applicable
	Alternative 2	Minor to Moderate impact	Construction BMP to reduce impacts of construction noise during work are required
Land Use and Planning			
	Alternative 1	No to Negligible impact	Not applicable
	Alternative 2	No to Negligible impact	Any rezoning necessary under local requirements would take place through the City's standard zoning process
Transportation			
	Alternative 1	No to Negligible impact	Not applicable
	Alternative 2	Minor impact (short term), Minor impact (positive long term)	Not applicable
Public Health and Safety			
	Alternative 1	No to Negligible impact	Not applicable

Alternative 2	Minor impact	Any work requiring disturbance of Asbestos Containing Materials must be undertaken by properly licensed contractors; hazardous materials must be properly disposed
Demolition		
Alternative 1	No to Negligible impact	Not applicable
Alternative 2	Moderate impact	Discovery and removal of site contamination in excess of IDNR requirements must be coordinated with the IDNR, BMP to prevent the release of soil or groundwater contaminants to surrounding properties and in transit must be used; salvage or recycling of uncontaminated building components should be considered as practicable
Cumulative Impact		
Alternative 1	Minor impact	Not applicable
Alternative 2	Minor to moderate impact	Implementation of applicable City regulations, air quality monitoring, use of BMP for control of fugitive dust, sedimentation and erosion, and noise, appropriate permitting, and coordination with IDNR and SHPO are expected to limit negative impacts

5. AFFECTED ENVIRONMENT AND IMPACTS

Chapter 5 describes the existing environmental conditions that may be affected by the proposed FEMA grant funding being applied towards construction of a new Parkade. The environmental impacts of the No Action Alternative were also analyzed.

This chapter also describes the potential environmental consequences of the proposed alternatives by comparing them with the potentially affected environmental components. The proposed activity was also evaluated against existing environmental documentation on current and planned actions and information on anticipated future projects to determine the potential for cumulative impacts. The potential for significant environmental consequences was evaluated utilizing the context and intensity considerations as defined in CEQ regulations for implementing the procedural provisions of NEPA (40 CFR 1508.27).

5.1 PHYSICAL RESOURCES

5.1.1 Geology and Soils

The topography of the proposed Parkade is located in a substantially developed area of Cedar Rapids. Because the proposed site is located within a highly developed portion of the City, soil classifications have not been compiled for the area and therefore are not available.

5.1.1.1 Alternative 1 - No Action

The No Action Alternative would have no significant effect on geology or soils. There would be no construction, improvements, or ground disturbance associated with this alternative. The existing parking facility and pavement would remain in place to minimize erosion from the site.

5.1.1.2 Alternative 2 - Proposed Action

The construction of the proposed Parkade would result in temporary disturbance of surface soils in the project area. Implementation of Best Management Practices (BMP) identified in a Storm Water Pollution Prevention Plan (SWPPP), as required by National Pollution Discharge Elimination System (NPDES) regulations, would minimize soil erosion and loss until construction is complete and the site is permanently stabilized. Therefore, the Proposed Action would have no significant impact to geology and soils. Non-structural BMP may utilize the minimization of disturbance, preservation of natural vegetation and re-vegetation of exposed slopes and soils to minimize erosion and to stabilize slopes. Structural erosion control BMP includes the placement of mulch or grass and the covering of stockpiles. Structural sediment control BMP includes silt fencing and sediment traps. The Applicant will be required to coordinate with IDNR for any required NPDES permits as the project site is greater than 1 acre in size (also see 5.14 Coordination and Permitting). See 5.7 Hazardous Substances for additional discussion regarding potential soil contamination.

5.1.2 Air Quality

The 1990 Clean Air Act, its amendments, and NEPA require that air quality impacts be addressed in the preparation of environmental documents. The U.S. Environmental Protection Agency (EPA) established National Ambient Air Quality Standards (NAAQS) for six "criteria" pollutants; carbon monoxide (CO), nitrogen dioxide (NO2), ozone (O3), particulate matter (PM10 and PM2.5), sulfur dioxide (SO2) and lead (Pb), and define the allowable concentrations that may be reached but not exceeded in a given time period to protect human health (primary standard) and welfare (secondary standard) with a reasonable margin of safety.

Primary and secondary standards for NAAQS have been established for most of the criteria pollutants which are detailed in Table 5-1: National Ambient Air Quality Standards, below. The EPA is authorized to designate those locations that have not met the NAAQS as non-attainment and to classify these non-attainment areas according to their degree of severity. Attainment pertains to the compliance/violation of any of the National Ambient Air Quality Standards (NAAQS) for the six criteria pollutants mentioned above. Each year, states are required to submit an annual monitoring network plan to EPA. The network plans provide for the creation and maintenance of monitoring stations, in accordance with EPA monitoring requirements specified in 40 CFR Part 58. The State of Iowa's most recent Monitoring Network Plan was approved by EPA Region 7 in December 2010.

The Linn County Public Health Department, Air Quality Division, is authorized by the EPA to implement and enforce the Clean Air Act and the county's code on Air Quality. The Linn County Air Quality Division maintains a network of instruments and devices located throughout the Cedar Rapids metropolitan area to monitor ambient air. The nearest Air Quality Monitoring System location is Scottish Rite Temple at 616 A Avenue NE in Cedar Rapids, within a half mile from the proposed Cedar Rapids Convention Complex Parkade. As of March 30, 2012, the only area within the State of Iowa considered a non-attainment area for the six criteria pollutants is Pottawattamie County.

Table 5-1: National Ambient Air Quality Standards

Pollutant	Primary Standards		Secondary Standards	
	Level	Averaging Time	Level	Averaging Time
Carbon Monoxide	9 ppm (10 mg/m^3)	8-hour	None	
	35 ppm (40 mg/m^3)	1-hour		
Lead	0.15 mg/m^3	Rolling 3-Month Average	Same as Primary	
Nitrogen Dioxide	53 ppb	Annual (Arithmetic Average)	Same as Primary	
	100 ppb	1-hour	None	
Particulate Matter (PM$_{10}$)	150 mg/m^3	24-hour	Same as Primary	
Particulate Matter (PM$_{2.5}$)	15 mg/m^3	Annual (Arithmetic Average)	Same as Primary	

	35 mg/m^3	24-hour	Same as Primary	
Ozone	0.075 ppm (2008 std)	8-hour	Same as Primary	
	0.08 ppm (1997 std)	8-hour	Same as Primary	
	0.12 ppm	1-hour	Same as Primary	
Sulfur Dioxide	0.03 ppm (1971 std)	Annual (Arithmetic Average)	0.5 ppm	3-hour
	0.14 ppm (1971 std)	24-hour		
	75 ppb	1-hour	None	

Source: USEPA 2011a

5.1.2.1 Alternative 1 - No Action

The No Action Alternative would not affect air quality beyond the existing conditions which are within regulatory standards. No construction activities would occur with the selection of the No Action Alternative. Vehicle emissions from the various apparatus may be higher as a result of continued dispersion between current parking lot locations. The impact of these potential higher emissions would remain incremental and would be difficult to measure meaningfully in the short term.

5.1.2.2 Alternative 2 - Proposed Action

Under this alternative, the Proposed Action would require the excavation of soil for the construction of the Cedar Rapids Convention Complex Parkade, thereby short-term emissions of criteria pollutants are anticipated during the construction phase. Construction equipment and personal vehicles would generate exhaust emissions; including NO2 and CO.

The operation of motor vehicles on unpaved surfaces and the use of earthmoving equipment may also generate particulate matter. The moving and handling of soil during construction would increase the potential for emissions of fugitive dust; however, any deterioration of air quality would be a localized, short-term condition that would be discontinued upon project completion and disturbed soils would be stabilized or permanently covered. The proposed action would require approximately 18 months of construction and heavy equipment including; bulldozers, scrapers, and backhoes.

Construction activities would be required to minimize fugitive dust emissions through watering, controlling entrainment of dust by vehicles, and/or other measures to reduce the disturbance of particulate matter. Increases in ambient concentrations of the criteria pollutants resulting from heavy equipment would be minor and Federal or State air quality attainment levels would not be exceeded. The Proposed Action is expected to have no long-term adverse impacts on the air quality of the area.

Mitigation

- Construction activities would be required to minimize fugitive dust emissions through watering, controlling entrainment of dust by vehicles, and/or other measures to reduce the disturbance of particulate matter.

- During site preparation and construction, the contractor would:
  - Minimize land disturbance;
  - Suppress dust on traveled paths that are not paved through wetting, use of watering trucks, chemical dust suppressants, or other reasonable precautions to prevent dust from entering ambient air;
  - Cover trucks when hauling soil;
  - Minimize soil track-out by washing or cleaning truck wheels before leaving the construction site;
  - Stabilize the surface of soil piles; and
  - Create wind breaks.
- During site restoration, the contractor would:
  - Revegetate any disturbed land not used with native species in accordance with Executive Order (EO) 13112
  - Remove unused material, and
  - Remove soil piles via covered trucks.

5.1.3 Climate Change

Climate change encompasses changes in precipitation, sea level, temperature and other climatic variables including natural cycles and the climatic changes attributed to human actions on the environment. The EPA identifies the climate change largely associated with human actions as "abrupt climate change" occurring over decades to distinguish it from that which occurs gradually over centuries or millennia. In 2010 the CEQ issued draft guidance for Federal agencies to consider climate change in NEPA documentation. The guidance uses the EPA-defined threshold for mandatory greenhouse gas (GHG) emission reporting of 25,000 metric tons per year as a level where NEPA documents determine whether a quantitative analysis is required. This threshold is equivalent to the energy needed to power 2,300 homes for a year or the emissions from 4,600 passenger vehicles per year (USEPA, 2009). FEMA has determined that the actions considered in this EA are incremental changes compared to the pre-disaster condition and the overall effects are expected to be significantly below this threshold.[1] The majority of GHG emissions result from industry, heating and cooling of buildings, and automobile non-point sources.

Average temperatures in Cedar Rapids reach a low in January between 15° and 20° Fahrenheit (F) and a high in July between 70° and 75° F. Peak precipitation is June through August which on average ranges between 4 and 5 inches per month. January and February tend to be when the average low precipitation of about 1 inch can be expected. However, average snowfall peaks in December to January of between 8 and 9 inches per month. Average morning humidity in Cedar Rapids tends to be around 80% with higher humidity June through September with average peak morning humidity in August around 90%. Average afternoon humidity between

---

[1] The Draft EA developed by consultants on behalf of FEMA Region X for the Veronia K-12 School Project includes a quantification of GHG. This accounting found that the new 135,000 sf school with 18,000 sf in outbuilding space to be built to LEED Platinum standards would result in the emission of 152 metric tons per year of GHG, significantly below the EPA threshold. This draft EA can be found on FEMA's website at; http://www.fema.gov/library/viewRecord.do?id=4351.

April and October tends to be below 65% with average afternoon humidity peaks in December and January of over 70%.

Between 1958 and 2007 amounts of very heavy precipitation has increased by 31% in the Upper Midwest encompassing Iowa, Missouri, Minnesota, Michigan, Illinois, Indiana, Ohio, and Wisconsin. During the same period, the Upper Midwest experienced a 27% in the average number of days with heavy precipitation defined as the heaviest 1% of all events. Heavy downpours currently occurring one time in 20 years on average are projected to increase in frequency between 10% and 25% through the 2090s (USGCRP, 2009).

Average temperatures in the United States have increased more than 2° F in the last 50 years. Average temperatures in Iowa and portions of surrounding states are projected to increase by another 4° to 6° F, under low-emission models, or 8° to 10° F, under high-emission models, by the end of the century. Under current projections, Iowa can anticipate increases in flooding, heat waves, droughts, invasive plant and insect species, and insect-borne diseases (USGCRP, 2009). While data needed to predict specific events and the full range of climate impacts are still being developed, enough data is available to suggest that climatic events, such as severe storms, will be localized and will be increasingly unpredictable.

Embodied energy is a concept in measuring sustainability that has been used since the early-1970s to account for the energy, often in terms of carbon, invested into an existing material or structure. Another measure of sustainability is life-cycle or cradle-to-grave analysis which accounts for the extraction, manufacture, distribution, use, and eventual disposal of materials. While resources exist to quantify embodied energy or life cycle analysis, the calculations were not prepared by the City for the options presented in this EA.

5.1.3.1 Alternative 1 - No Action

Under the No Action Alternative 1, FEMA would not fund demolition, debris removal, and new construction activities for Parkade. No impact or change to the overall embodied energy or energy usage is expected.

5.1.3.2 Alternative 2 - Proposed Action

Applicant proposes to demolish, remove original damaged surface parking lot and construct a new Parkade facility. Proposed parking structure will be multi-levels with 460 parking spaces; potential to add another floor with an additional 75 parking spaces. Increase in energy usage is anticipated to be a negligible to minor impact. The construction of the parking structure will represent a considerable increased investment of embodied energy represented by the quantities of concrete and metal construction materials.

Salvage or recycling of uncontaminated debris such as crushing concrete for future use as aggregate or other uses should be implemented to mitigate the impact of demolition. Such opportunities are expected to reduce the impact of the demolition to the human environment through reducing wasted embodied energy and the premature opening and closing of cells at the landfill. Reuse of materials on-site could further reduce incremental impacts by reducing transportation of materials.

5.2 WATER RESOURCES

5.2.1 Water Quality

Congress enacted the Federal Water Pollution Control Act in 1948 which was reorganized and expanded in 1972 and became known as the Clean Water Act (CWA) in 1977, as amended. The CWA regulates discharge of pollutants into water with sections falling under the jurisdiction of the U.S Army Corps of Engineers (USACE) and the EPA. Section 404 of the CWA establishes the USACE permit requirements for discharging dredged or fill materials into Waters of the United States and traditional navigable waterways. USACE regulation of activities within navigable waters is also authorized under the 1899 Rivers and Harbors Act. The USACE jurisdiction extends to tributaries and wetlands where a "significant nexus" exists between the resources as articulated in two recent Supreme Court decisions known as the SWANCC and Rapanos decisions. Under the National Pollution Discharge Elimination System (NPDES) the EPA regulates both point and non-point pollutant sources, including storm water and storm water runoff. Activities that disturb one acre of ground or more are required to apply for an NPDES permit through the Iowa Department of Natural Resources (IDNR) as authorized by the EPA. The Wild and Scenic Rivers Act is another regulatory framework related to water resources; however there are no designated wild and scenic rivers in the State of Iowa.

Cedar Rapids is further regulated by NPDES with a Municipal Separate Storm Sewer System (MS4) individual or general permit. MS4 permits require the City to develop and maintain a storm water management program (SWMP) to reduce contamination of storm water and limit contamination discharges.

5.2.1.1 Alternative 1 - No Action

Under the No Action Alternative 1, FEMA would not fund demolition and new construction activities for Parkade. Over time, the deteriorating parking lot facility has the potential for minor negative impacts on surface and ground water quality for Cedar River, surrounding wetlands, and ground water aquifers.

5.2.1.2 Alternative 2 - Proposed Action

Construction of the Parkade facility would disturb more than 1 acre of ground for the amount of excavation required to ensure stabilized soils, utilities, and associated site work. Ground disturbing activities 1 acre or greater requires the Applicant to prepare a Storm Water Pollution Prevention Plan (SWPPP) and to obtain and comply with a NPDES permit from the IDNR (also see 5.7 Coordination and Permits). All ground disturbing activities would require site and project appropriate sediment and erosion control Best Management Practices (BMP). Implementation of BMP and permit conditions would reduce the potential impact of this project to minor levels.

5.2.2 Wetlands

In addition to the CWA, Executive Order (EO) 11990 Protection of Wetlands requires Federal agencies to avoid, to the extent practicable, adverse impacts to wetlands. Under the CWA two types of authorization are available from the USACE for activities regulated under Section 404 of the Clean Water Act: general nationwide permits, which are issued for a specific category of similar activities and include nationwide permits defined in 33 CFR Part 30, and individual permits issued after review of the project, project alternative, and proposed mitigation.

The 1987 Corps of Engineers Wetlands Delineation Manual provides the technical guidelines in identifying and delineating wetlands. The Corps' manual requires the presence of all three parameters (greater than 50% dominance of hydrophytic vegetation, evidence of hydric soils, and presence of hydrologic indicators) for an area to be considered a wetland. The U.S. Fish and Wildlife Service (USFWS) maintains the National Wetlands Inventory (NWI) maps including conventional maps, downloadable digital map data, dynamic online maps[2] and geographic information system (GIS) data. Federal actions within identified wetlands require the Federal agency to conduct an 8-Step process, which like NEPA, requires the evaluation of alternatives prior to funding the action. FEMA's regulations on conducting 8-Step processes are contained in 44 CFR Part 9.5.

5.2.2.1 Alternative 1 - No Action

Under the No Action Alternative, FEMA would not fund demolition, debris removal, and new construction activities for the Parkade. Over time, the deteriorating abandoned facility has the potential for minor to moderate (i.e., measurable) negative impacts to surrounding wetlands.

5.2.2.2 Alternative 2 - Proposed Action

A review of the National Wetlands Inventory Map and site visit performed in March 29, 2012 indicates that no wetlands are located on or near the proposed site. The Contractor is required to implement best management practices to reduce or eliminate runoff impacts during proposed construction activities of the Proposed Action.

5.2.3 Floodplain

EO 11988 (Floodplain Management) requires that a Federal agency avoid direct or indirect support of development within the 100-year floodplain whenever there is a practicable alternative. FEMA uses Flood Insurance Rate Maps (FIRM) to identify the floodplains for the National Flood Insurance Program (NFIP). Federal actions within the 100-year floodplain, or 500-year floodplain for critical actions, require the Federal agency to conduct an 8-Step process. This process, like NEPA, requires the evaluation of alternatives prior to funding the action. FEMA's regulations on conducting 8-Step processes are contained in 44 CFR Part 9.5. Cedar Rapids, Iowa is a participant in the NFIP with updated FIRMs promulgated in April of 2010. FIRM Panels 1901870020B dated December 15, 1982 covering the existing Lots 24/26 facilities addressed in this EA were in effect as of the 2008 floods. Revised FIRMs were issued April 5, 2010 with Panel 19113C0410D encompassing the same facilities. The proposed site for the construction of the Parkade facility is not located in the 100-year floodplain.

---

[2] U.S. Fish and Wildlife Service National Wetland Inventory Geospatial Wetlands Digital Data is available at; http://www.fws.gov/wetlands/data/index.html

---

5.2.3.1 Alternative 1 - No Action

Under the No Action Alternative no additional work would take place beyond the emergency activities already undertaken.

5.2.3.2 Alternative 2 - Proposed Action

Construction of the proposed Parkade facility would not impact the 100-year floodplain.

5.3 BIOLOGICAL RESOURCES

5.3.1 Protected Species and Habitat

The Endangered Species Act (ESA) of 1973 establishes a Federal program to conserve, protect, and restore threatened or endangered plants and animals and their habitats. ESA specifically charges Federal agencies with the responsibility of using their authority to conserve threatened or endangered species. Biological studies consisting of literature review and map documentation were performed. A site visit was conducted on March 29, 2012.

All Federal agencies must ensure any action they authorize, fund, or carry out is not likely to jeopardize the continued existence of an endangered or threatened species or result in the destruction of critical habitat for these species. EO 13112 prohibits Federal agencies from funding, authorizing, or carrying out actions that are likely to cause or promote the introduction or spread of invasive species in the United States.

Table 5-2: Federally Protected Species of Linn County, Iowa

Common Name	Scientific Name	Status	Potential Occurrence at Site	Reason
Indiana bat	*Myotis sodalist*	Endangered	No	No habitat
Western prairie fringed orchid	*Platanthera praeclara*	Threatened	No	No habitat
Prairie bush clover	*Lespedeza leptostachya*	Threatened	No	No habitat

5.3.1.1 Alternative 1 - No Action

The No Action Alternative would not impact vegetation or wildlife in the project area. No construction activities would occur with the selection of the No Action Alternative.

5.3.1.2 Alternative 2 - Proposed Action

The impact of the proposed FEMA funded construction of the Parkade upon threatened and endangered species has been determined to be "no effect". No remaining native habitats are present on the site as the site had been developed commercially since at least 1884. Re-vegetation of the property at the end of construction is expected to consist of native plantings and consistent with previous City landscape architecture and design.

Coordination with the City's forestry department and/or the IDNR for native species should take place if a listing of approved plant species has not already been established.

FEMA reviewed lists from both U.S. Fish and Wildlife Service (USFWS) and the Iowa Department of Natural Resources (IDNR) for threatened and endangered species with potential to occur in Linn County. It was determined from documentation review and a field visit to the project area, that threatened or endangered species identified as having potential to occur in Linn County were not present in the area or would be impacted by the project.

5.4 CULTURAL RESOURCES

In addition to review under NEPA, consideration of impacts to cultural resources is mandated under Section 106 of the National Historic Preservation Act (NHPA), as amended and implemented by 36 CFR Part 800. Requirements include the identification of significant cultural resources that may be impacted by the undertaking. Cultural resources are prehistoric and historic sites, structures, districts, buildings, objects, artifacts, or any other physical evidence of human activity considered important to a culture, subculture, or community for scientific, traditional, religious, or other reasons.

Only those cultural resources determined to be potentially significant under NHPA are subject to protection from adverse impacts resulting from an undertaking. To be considered significant, a cultural resource must meet one or more of the criteria established by the National Park Service that would make that resource eligible for inclusion in the National Register of Historic Places (NRHP). The term "eligible for inclusion in the NRHP" includes all properties that meet the NRHP listing criteria, which are specified in the Department of Interior regulations Title 36, Part 60.4 and NRHP Bulletin 15. Sites not yet evaluated may be considered potentially eligible for inclusion in the NRHP and, as such, are afforded the same regulatory consideration as nominated properties. Whether prehistoric, historic, or traditional, significant cultural resources are referred to as "historic properties."

For the purposes of this analysis, the term "Area of Potential Effects" (APE) as defined under cultural resources legislation, defines all historic properties that could be affected by each Alternatives' actions and encompasses areas requiring ground disturbance (e.g. areas of grading, cut and fill, etc) associated with the proposed Federal undertaking. For No Action Alternative, neither the demolition of the original facility, nor the construction of a new facility in conjunction with a Federal undertaking would occur; therefore Section 106 review would not apply. For Proposed Action Alternative evaluated in this EA, FEMA has determined that the APE for this undertaking for archaeological resources is limited to the areas of ground disturbance necessary for demolition, excavation, construction, utility connections, access, and staging that would be confined to Lots 24/26, the intersecting alley, and the public right-of-way. The APE for this undertaking regarding historic structures extends to the buildings and structures within the block and those that surround the block, including the Chicago, Milwaukee and St. Paul Railroad Corridor that joins 4th Street Railroad Corridor to the Northeast.

5.4.1 Historic Properties

FEMA has considered the potential for these Alternatives to affect historic structures. Various sources were checked to determine if any previously identified historic properties are located within the APE for both Alternatives proposed for this undertaking and to determine the potential for the APE to contain previously unidentified historic properties. This review included the NRHP and National Historic Landmarks Databases, and the Office of the State Archaeologist's (OSA) I-Sites GIS and Database, historic maps and aerial photographs available through the Iowa Geographic Map Server at Iowa State University and the University of Iowa Libraries' Iowa Digital Library.

The site identified as Lots 24/26 were developed in the 1980s and 1990s following demolition of buildings on the site as evidenced by historic aerials. Therefore, Lots 24/26 do not meet the 50-year criterion required by the NRHP listing criteria, or the level of exceptional importance required by Criteria Consideration G, for properties that have achieved significance within the past 50 years. The footprint of the intersecting alley likely dates to the early development of downtown Cedar Rapids, and infilling the alley is the type of activity that has the potential to compromise the integrity of an NRHP listed or eligible historic district, should a district be present. The Parkade is proposed to be connected to the Cedar Rapids Convention Complex to the North across 1st Avenue E. The Convention Complex does not meet the 50-year criterion required by the NRHP listing criteria, or the level of exceptional importance required by Criteria Consideration G. Installing a skywalk within the boundaries of a listed or eligible historic district is the type of activity that has the potential to compromise the integrity of an historic district, should one be present. However, the proposed project is not within the boundaries of a district that is listed in or has been determined eligible for listing in the NRHP. Furthermore, previous historic and architectural surveys of Cedar Rapids have identified a collection of NRHP individually eligible buildings downtown Cedar Rapids, but suggest that due to losses and intrusions, the potential for an NRHP eligible historic district downtown Cedar Rapids is low.

The former Iowa Theatre Building, now home to the local community theatre group, Theatre Cedar Rapids was completed in 1928, and has been determined eligible for listing in the NRHP by FEMA in consultation with the State Historical Society of Iowa/State Historic Preservation Office (SHPO). The Iowa Theatre Building is located to the southwest of the proposed parking structure within the city block, and the proposed parking ramp would abut the rear elevation of the Iowa Theatre Building. The former Cedar Rapids Post Office and Public Building, constructed in 1908, located at 305 2nd Avenue SE in the block southeast of the project area was listed in the NRHP in 1982.

Several other buildings within the APE have previously been evaluated as being potentially eligible for listing in the NRHP. In April, 1997, Marlys, A. Svendsen, Svendsen, Tyler, Inc. of Sarona, Wisconsin completed *Historical and Architectural Reconnaissance Survey Report for the Downtown and Industrial Corridors in Cedar Rapids, Iowa* for the City of Cedar Rapids Department of Development and the Cedar Rapids Historic Preservation Commission. As a result of the referenced survey, MS. Svendsen determined that the Muskvaki Block, c. 1900, formerly the Dragon Restaurant at 325-329 2nd Avenue SE, directly southeast of the project area is potentially NRHP eligible. The surrounding blocks also contain multiple properties that were determined potentially individually eligible for listing in the NRHP in the referenced survey. A map that identifies the locations of NRHP listed and potentially eligible properties, page 76, and *Appendix I: Potential National Register Eligible Properties* extracted from the survey report are attached for reference.

5.4.1.1 Alternative 1 - No Action

No Action Alternative would result in neither the demolition of the original facility, or the construction of a new facility in conjunction with a Federal undertaking; therefore Section 106 review would not apply.

5.4.1.2 Alternative 2 - Proposed Action

Proposed Action Alternative, Applicant's preferred option, would require the demolition of the original facility and the construction of the proposed new facility to be located on roughly the Northeastern half of the block bounded by 1st Avenue E on the Northwest, 2nd Avenue SE on the Southeast, 3rd Street SE on the Southwest and the Chicago, Milwaukee and St. Paul Railroad Corridor that joins 4th Street Railroad Corridor to the Northeast.

As noted, Lots 24/26 do not meet the NRHP listing criteria. Therefore, demolition of the surface parking will not constitute adverse effects to historic structures. As stated above, the proposed project is not within the boundaries of a district that is listed in or has been determined eligible for listing in the NRHP, and previous surveys suggest that the potential for an eligible historic district is low. Therefore, it is not anticipated that the intersecting alley would be identified as being within the boundaries of a potentially eligible historic district. Therefore the Proposed Action Alternative, and infilling within the alley system should not constitute adverse effects to historic structures. The Parkade is proposed to be connected to the Cedar Rapids Convention Complex to the North across 1st Avenue E. The Convention Complex does not meet the 50-year criterion required by the NRHP listing criteria, or the level of exceptional importance required by Criteria Consideration G, for properties that have achieved significance within the past 50 years. Installing a skywalk within the boundaries of a potential or listed historic district is the type of activity that has the potential to compromise the integrity of a listed or eligible historic district, should one be present. As stated above, previous historic and architectural surveys of Cedar Rapids have identified a collection of NRHP individually eligible buildings downtown Cedar Rapids, but suggest that due to losses and intrusions, the potential for an NRHP eligible historic district downtown Cedar Rapids is low.

It is not anticipated that construction of the new facility in Proposed Action Alternative will result in adverse effects to adjacent NRHP listed and eligible historic structures as the proposed facility would be similar in size, scale and massing to the historic structures within the APE, and the overall character of the area.

In the event that Proposed Action Alternative is approved, FEMA will evaluate the properties within the APE for eligibility for listing in the NRHP, assess the effects of the undertaking on historic properties within the APE and consult with the SHPO. It is not anticipated that consultation would result in a determination of adverse effects to historic structures.

An adverse effect is found when an undertaking may alter, directly or indirectly, any of the characteristics of a historic property that qualify the property for inclusion in the NRHP in a manner that would diminish the integrity of a property's location, design, setting, materials, workmanship, feeling or association. Through FEMA's application of the criteria of adverse effect and consultation with the SHPO, if it is determined that Proposed

Action Alternative may constitute adverse effects to historic standing structures within the APE, FEMA would initiate adverse effects consultation with the SHPO and other consulting parties, and through the development of a Memorandum of Agreement (MOA) under Section 106, develop and evaluate alternatives or modifications to the undertaking that could avoid, minimize or mitigate adverse effects on historic properties. Through resolution of adverse effects, FEMA would make information regarding the undertaking and effected historic properties available to the public and provide an opportunity for the public to express their views on resolving adverse effects of the undertaking on historic structures. The resultant MOA would evidence FEMA's compliance with its statutory responsibilities under Section 106 of the NHPA.

5.4.2 Archaeological Resources

FEMA has considered the potential for the Alternatives to affect archaeological resources. Various sources were checked to determine if any previously identified historic properties, including archeological sites are located within the APE of these Alternatives and to determine the potential for the APE to contain previously unidentified historic properties. This review included the NRHP and National Historic Landmarks Databases, and the OSA I-Sites GIS and Database, historic maps and aerial photographs available through the Iowa Geographic Map Server at Iowa State University and the University of Iowa Libraries' Iowa Digital Library. According to the master inventory of archaeological sites in Iowa, no previously recorded archaeological sites are located within the APE; however, seven previously identified sites are located within 1 mile of the APE. According to the NRCS Web Soil Survey, the soil data for this parcel has not been compiled. The site is located in a developed urban environment. According to the available Sanborn Fire Insurance Maps, the block previously contained a variety of commercial properties and has been redeveloped over time. The site is considered moderately sensitive for the presence of pre-historic (Native American) archaeological deposits.

5.4.2.1 Alternative 1 - No Action

No Action Alternative would result in neither the demolition of the original facility, or the construction of a new facility in conjunction with a Federal undertaking; therefore Section 106 review would not apply. The No Action Alternative would not include any demolition activities within Lots 24/26 and the intersecting alley, nor any construction activities for a new facility, therefore no ground disturbing activities would occur, and no archeological resources that may be present would be affected with the selection of No Action Alternative. Additionally, No Action Alternative would not result in removal of the concrete and asphaltic parking surfaces that cover the site, thus continuing to provide protection for any intact archaeological resources that may be present.

5.4.2.2 Alternative 2 - Proposed Action

Proposed Action Alternative, Applicant's preferred option, would require the demolition of the original facility and the construction of a new facility that would be confined to Lots 24/ 26, the intersecting alley and the public right-of-way. There are no previously recorded archaeological sites located within the APE of Proposed Action Alternative; however, seven previously identified sites are located within 1 mile of the APE. According to the Web Soil Survey, the soil data for this parcel has not been compiled. The site is located in a developed urban environment.

According to the available Sanborn Fire Insurance Maps, the block previously contained a variety of commercial properties and has been redeveloped over time. The site is considered moderately sensitive for the presence of pre-historic (Native American) archaeological deposits; however, construction would not notably disturb more ground than was disturbed by previous construction and demolitions on the site. Therefore, FEMA will not recommend a Phase 1 Archaeological Survey in advance of the proposed construction, or monitoring by an archaeologist who meets the Secretary of the Interior's (SOI) Professional Qualifications Standards during the demolition and excavation.

Demolition, consisting of removal of concrete and asphaltic surfaces on Lots 24/26 and the intersecting alley would not likely affect archaeological resources as the demolition would not disturb more ground than was disturbed by their installation. Therefore for Proposed Action Alternative, the demolition of the original facility should not affect archaeological resources. It is not anticipated that construction of the Parkade will result in effects to historic archaeological resources as the proposed facility would be confined to the block within a developed urban environment and would not notably disturb more ground than was disturbed by previous construction and demolitions on the site. Though, it is not unreasonable to assume that historic period archaeological sites consisting of building foundations and/or other features that may represent significant intact *in-situ* cultural deposits that could potentially advance knowledge of 19th century life-ways in Iowa may be encountered. It is not likely that an archaeological site that would meet the NRHP listing criteria would be encountered.

In the event that Proposed Action Alternative is approved, FEMA will consult with the SHPO on the effects of the undertaking on archaeological resources.

Due to the potential for archaeological discoveries on the site, FEMA would condition approval of the undertaking with the following discovery clause: In the event that any archaeological deposits (soils, features, or any other remnants of human activity) are uncovered during the undertaking, this project shall be halted, the Applicant shall stop all work immediately in the vicinity of the discovery and take reasonable measures to avoid or minimize harm to the finds. The City will inform IHSEMD immediately, will secure all archaeological findings and restrict access to the area. IHSEMD shall notify FEMA and FEMA will consult with the SHPO and the State Archaeologist of Iowa. Work in sensitive areas may not resume until consultations are completed or until an archaeologist who meets the Secretary of the Interior's Professional Qualification Standards determines the extent and historical significance of the discovery. Work may not resume at or around the delineated archaeological deposit until the Applicant is notified by IHSEMD.

If archaeological resources are encountered and subsequently recommended eligible for listing in the NRHP by the SOI qualified archaeologist, construction activities on the site shall halt until FEMA has re-opened and concluded consultation with the SHPO. In the event that NRHP eligible archaeological resources may be identified and the project cannot be modified to avoid adverse effects to archaeological resources, FEMA would initiate adverse effects consultation with the SHPO and other consulting parties, and through the development of a MOA under Section 106, develop and evaluate alternatives or modifications to the undertaking that could avoid, minimize or mitigate adverse effects on historic archaeological resources. Through resolution of adverse effects, FEMA would make information regarding the undertaking and effected historic properties available to the public and provide an opportunity for the public to express their views on resolving adverse effects of the undertaking on historic standing structures. The resultant MOA would evidence FEMA's compliance with its statutory responsibilities under Section 106 of the NHPA.

5.5 SOCIOECONOMIC CONSIDERATIONS

5.5.1 Environmental Justice

On February 11, 1994, President Clinton signed Executive Order (EO) 12898, *"Federal Actions to Address Environmental Justice in Minority Populations and Low-Income Populations."* The EO directs Federal agencies to focus attention on human health and environmental conditions in minority and/or low-income communities. Its goals are to achieve environmental justice, fostering non-discrimination in Federal programs that substantially affect human health or the environment, and to give minority or low-income communities greater opportunities for public participation in and access to public information on matters relating to human health and the environment. Also identified and addressed, as appropriate are, disproportionately high and adverse human health, or environmental effects of its programs, policies, and activities on minority populations and low-income populations in the United States.

The proposed Cedar Rapids Convention Complex Parkade is located within Census Tract 19. Select demographic data used in this analysis is contained in Appendix A, Figure 9. Census Tract 19 has minority populations (16.8%) higher than the proportion of the City as a whole (12%). Census Tract 19 has lower median ages for men and for women than the City as a whole. Census Tract 19 has a significantly lower proportion of elderly residents than the City as a whole.

5.5.1.1 Alternative 1 - No Action

The No Action Alternative would have no impact to the socioeconomics of the local area because no construction activity would occur in the short term.

5.5.1.2 Alternative 2 - Proposed Action

Construction of the proposed Parkade under this alternative would result in a positive impact with an influx of construction workers needed for the approximately 18 months of construction activities. Construction personnel would provide short-term benefits to the local businesses, which would include the purchase of food, gas, and other services. The Proposed Action would not displace or adversely affect any nearby residents or minority populations during the construction phase. Thereby, construction of the proposed Cedar Rapids Convention Complex Parkade is anticipated to be beneficial by centralizing and improving parking services to the area. Other potential benefits are associated with additional retail, office, or other work-space associated with the ground-level commercial uses.

5.5.2 Noise

As a result of the human health and welfare impacts of uncontrolled noise, the Noise Control Act was enacted in 1972; however EPA does not have regulatory authority governing noise in local communities. In 1982, the EPA shifted Federal noise control policy and transferred the primary responsibility of regulating noise to state

---

and local governments. The Noise Control Act of 1972 and the Quiet Communities Act of 1978 were not rescinded by Congress and remain in effect.

The term "noise" is considered unwanted or nuisance sound and is typically measured in decibels (dB). The day-night average sound level (Ldn) is the 24-hour average sound level, in dB, obtained after the addition of 10 dB to the sound levels occurring between 10 p.m. and 7 a.m. and is used by agencies for estimating sound impacts and establishing guidelines for compatible land uses. The U.S. Department of Housing and Urban Development (HUD) regulations set acceptable noise levels at 65 Ldn or less (24 CFR Part 51). The EPA identifies a 24-hour exposure level of 70 decibels (dB) as the level of environmental noise which will prevent any measurable hearing loss over a lifetime. Likewise, levels of 55 dB outdoors and 45 dB indoors are identified as preventing activity interference and annoyance (e.g., spoken conversation, sleeping, working, recreation). The levels represent averages of acoustic energy over long periods of time such as 8 hours or 24 hours rather than single events. Table 5-3, below, presents some common construction equipment with their estimated noise levels and levels at various distances. Noise regulations take into account sensitive receptors which are populations or land uses that may be impacted to a greater extent by increases in ambient noise levels. Sensitive receptors generally include museums, libraries, day care centers, schools, hospitals, and places of worship, among others.

Table 5-3: Estimated Sound Levels for Construction Equipment and Attenuation at Various Distances

Equipment	Typical Noise Level (dBA) at 50 ft. from Source[1]	Estimate at 100 ft.	Estimate at 200 ft.	Estimate at 500 ft.	Estimate at 1,000 ft.
Air Compressor	81	75	69	61	55
Backhoe	80	74	68	60	54
Concrete Mixer	85	79	73	65	59
Dozer	85	79	73	65	59
Generator	81	75	69	61	55
Loader	85	79	73	65	59
Paver	89	83	77	69	63
Pneumatic Tool	85	79	73	65	59
Pump	76	70	64	56	50
Saw	76	70	64	56	50
Shovel	82	76	70	62	56
Truck	88	82	76	68	62

Source: FHWA 2006

5.5.2.1 Alternative 1 - No Action

The No Action Alternative would not affect noise levels within the proposed project area or the surrounding community. No construction activities would occur with the selection of the No Action Alternative.

5.5.2.2 Alternative 2 - Proposed Action

Sensitive noise receptors have been identified in the area including the Cedar Rapids Museum of Art, the Carl and Mary Koehler History Center, St. John the Baptist Church, and Grace Episcopal Church. The Museum of Art is the nearest receptor at approximately 300 feet from the proposed site.

The Proposed Action would result in temporary increases in noise levels in the vicinity of the project area for the construction of the proposed project. Construction activities would require approximately 18 months of construction and the use of heavy equipment. Best Management Practices to minimize noise impacts to the two sensitive noise receptors are required. According to the Center for Environmental Excellence by the American Association of State Highway and Transportation Officials (AASHTO), BMPs for noise reduction include (AASHTO 2009);

- Early and frequent communication with the public;
- Planning noisier activities and equipment usage for mid-morning to mid-afternoon;
- Planning site access and staging to minimize or eliminate "back-up alarm" noise;
- Limiting equipment on site to only what is necessary;
- Imposing seasonal limitation on construction noise as spring and fall are critical times when windows are left open in residential areas;
- Using newer, "low-noise" models of equipment;
- Limiting construction activities to daylight hours;
- And, shift work to weekends rather than weeknights.

Once construction activities are completed, noise levels should return to pre-project levels. Applying BMPs for construction noise reduction is expected to minimize the short-term adverse impacts of the project. FEMA has determined that the proposed action is expected to have no long-term adverse impacts on the noise quality of the area.

5.5.3 Land Use and Planning

The Cedar Rapids Community Development Department coordinates planning activities in Cedar Rapids and advises the City Council, other departments, other non-City agencies, and private stakeholders on issues of development and planning within the City. Cedar Rapids adopted the current comprehensive plan in 1999 which established the community's priorities including vision, objectives, and goals through 2030. See 5.5.4 Transportation for metropolitan transportation planning discussion. Land-use and zoning regulations are administered and enforced by Cedar Rapids. Based on the review of the historical information in the Phase I Environmental Site Assessment, the Lots 24/26 site has been developed since at least 1884 with commercial and retail establishments including hotels, restaurants, tailors, barbers, drug stores, laundry, new printing and movie theaters. The site has existed as a paved parking lot since the 1990's.

5.5.3.1 Alternative 1 - No Action

Under the No Action Alternative, no impacts to land use are expected.

5.5.3.2 Alternative 2 - Proposed Action

Construction of the Parkade is expected to be consistent with the City's land use planning goals and would conform to existing zoning designations. The site is currently zoned C-4 which is designated for uses that accommodate business and residential uses that are characteristic of a downtown (Zoning Code, Sec. 32.03); see Appendix A, Figure 6.

5.5.4 Transportation

The Corridor Metropolitan Planning Organization (CMPO) is tasked under the 1973 Highway Act to coordinate metropolitan-wide transportation planning and investment. CMPO's most recent *Long Range Transportation Plan* (*LRTP*), consistent with SAFETEA-LU (current Federal transportation legislation), Clean Air Act (CAA), and Title VI of the 1964 Civil Rights Act, was adopted July 15, 2010.

5.5.4.1 Alternative 1 - No Action

Under the No Action Alternative, impacts to transportation are anticipated to remain unchanged from the post-disaster.

5.5.4.2 Alternative 2 - Proposed Action

Construction of the Parkade at the Lots 24/26 site is anticipated to have minor positive impacts to transportation services by increasing capacity of downtown parking facilities. Short term construction impacts to traffic on the surrounding roads are expected to be limited as the majority of the work is expected to be confined to the site. Traffic may be marginally impacted by construction equipment entering or leaving the site, however the impacts are expected to be partially mitigated by the urban street grid with the presence of alternate routes. Long term impacts may include increased traffic in the surrounding roads due to the availability of parking in a consolidated location.

5.5.6 Public Health and Safety

Hazardous wastes, as defined by the Resource Conservation and Recovery Act (RCRA), are defined as "a solid waste, or combination of solid wastes, which because of its quantity, concentration, or physical, chemical, or infectious characteristics may; (1) cause, or significantly contribute to, an increase in mortality or an increase in serious irreversible or incapacitating reversible illness or; (2) pose a substantial present or potential hazard to human health or the environment when improperly treated, stored, transported or disposed of or otherwise managed." Hazardous materials and wastes are regulated in Iowa by a combination of Federal and state laws. Federal regulations governing the assessment and disposal of hazardous wastes include RCRA, the RCRA Hazardous and Solid Waste Amendments, Comprehensive Environmental Response, Compensation and Liability Act (CERCLA), Solid Waste Act, and the Toxic Substances Control Act.

Radon (Rn) is a naturally occurring radioactive gas that is produced by the decay of uranium found within soil, rocks, and groundwater that accumulates in enclosed spaces such as the lowest level of buildings. The U.S.

Environmental Protection Agency (EPA) currently considers residential radon exposure at or above 4.0 pico Curies per liter (pCi/L) as a public health risk as an additional risk factor for development of lung cancer. The EPA provides a map for each county in the U.S. which shows the potential for elevated indoor radon levels, with Zone 1 having the highest potential for predicted average indoor screening levels greater than 4.0 pCi/L. According to the EPA's Map of Radon Zones, Linn County and the entire State of Iowa is mapped within Zone 1 (EPA, 2011b). Actual levels of radon can vary significantly from property to property, even within areas with high potential for elevated radon levels. Radon testing is the only way to determine actual radon levels within an enclosed space such as the lowest floor of a structure.

5.5.6.1 Alternative 1 - No Action

Under the No Action Alternative, no construction or demolition activities would take place. If soil or groundwater contamination is present, it would not be disturbed or discovered.

5.5.6.2 Alternative 2 - Proposed Action

Three known leaking underground storage tanks (LUST) have been identified in adjoining parcels associated with leaked diesel fuel and waste oil between 1995 and 1998; all three of which were identified during tank removal and reported to the IDNR. Multiple past and current LUST have also been identified up-gradient to the proposed project site. Cedar Rapids hired Terracon to conduct a Limited Site Assessment (LSI) resulting in the identification of multiple recognized environmental conditions (REC) on the site. The RECs include past land uses that including automotive filling and servicing, railroad use, coal storage, printing facilities, and laundry services. The survey found elevated levels of Benzo(a)pyrene, Arsnic, and motor oil exceeding statewide standards in the soil; groundwater samples were not taken and thus impacts to groundwater remain uncertain.

FEMA recommends that Cedar Rapids and its contractors follow the recommendations made in the Terracon report to minimize exposure to hazardous substances and to protect the public; see 5.5.7 Demolition for additional information. All hazardous substances must be properly transported and disposed of to minimize risk to workers and to the public in accordance with applicable Federal, State, and local laws.

With the movement and excavation of the shallow soils associated with the construction of this facility there is a potential for elevated concentrations of radon gas within the proposed building following construction. The project design should incorporate Radon-resistant construction appropriate to the site and overall project design as practicable; exact levels of radon present at the site can only be determined by site-specific testing. Radon-resistant construction techniques may vary for different foundations and site requirements, but in general include five key concepts:

- Gas Permeable Layer – Usually a 4-inch layer of clean gravel used beneath the slab or flooring system to allow soil-gas to move freely;
- Plastic sheeting – Polyethylene sheeting is placed on top of the gas permeable layer and under the slab to help prevent migration of the soil-gas from entering the facility;
- Vent Pipe – A PVC pipe runs from the gas permeable layer up through the structure to the roof to safely vent radon above the facility;
- Junction Box – An electrical junction box is installed in case an electrical venting fan is needed later; and,

- Sealing and Caulking – Openings in the concrete foundation are sealed to prevent soil-gas from entering the facility.

5.5.7 Demolition

The site for Lots 24/26 has been substantially developed thus any significant alteration to the site would require demolition activities. Demolition activities are regulated by Federal, State, and local laws ranging from local permits to licensure to appropriate disposal, see 5.5.5 for sub-surface discussion. Demolition debris is expected to be disposed of at the Cedar Rapids/Linn County Landfill #2 located at 1954 County Home Road which is authorized to receive non-friable asbestos.

If asbestos associated with previous land uses is discovered during demolition, site preparation, and foundation work is discovered, the Applicant must properly remove and dispose of the asbestos containing materials (ACM). Removal and disposal of ACM must be conducted in accordance with all applicable Federal, State, and local laws and documentation of proper handling and disposal must be submitted to FEMA. The depth of the 42 pier foundations as currently designed is 50 feet. Excavation will be limited to the removal of the existing pavement and the spoils from the foundations. The footprint of the excavation will extend approximately 3 feet past the property line on 4th street.

5.5.7.1 Alternative 1 - No Action

Under the No Action Alternative, no construction or demolition activities would take place.

5.5.7.2 Alternative 2 - Proposed Action

Construction of the Parkade at the Lots 24/26 site would require demolition of the existing surface parking facility and the spoils from foundations of structures formerly occupying the site.

If contamination in excess of reporting requirements is met, work must stop, the site must be stabilized, and the IDNR must be contacted at Field Office #1 (563-927-2640). Work within the sensitive area cannot resume until IDNR clean-up or containment requirements are met and IDNR personnel indicate that no further assessment is needed at the site of the discovery. Contaminated soils and material must be properly disposed of and surrounding properties protected from being impacted between disturbance and disposal; BMP to prevent release of contaminants while in transit to a permitted disposal site must be implemented.

5.6 CUMULATIVE IMPACTS

Cumulative effects are defined by the CEQ as the impact on the environment resulting from the incremental impacts of the evaluated actions when combined with other past, present, and reasonably foreseeable future actions, regardless of the source, such as Federal or non-Federal. Cumulative impacts can result from individually minor but collectively significant actions taken over time. Cedar Rapids is engaged in numerous flood recovery projects including private property acquisitions, residential and public building demolitions, relocation of public buildings, restoration of flood-impacted public facilities, and a City-desired flood protection system on both sides of the river.

Construction of the Parkade is expected to increase the short-term noise impacts to the downtown area with the use of heavy machinery and truck traffic. This impact combined with the construction work across 1st Avenue E on the Convention Center, the noise impacts of the heavily used 1st Avenue E corridor, and other large construction projects downtown is expected to be short-term; in the long term, the increase in noise is expected to be incremental and within the regulatory limits implemented by the City. The provision of significantly more parking spaces on the site may result in an increase the amount of vehicle traffic in the surrounding roads as well as a concentration of vehicle emissions. Emissions associated with operating the parking structure are incremental, but the potential concentration of vehicles at the site is anticipated to be a diversion of non-point sources from other areas in the City; Linn County Public Health will monitor the air quality impacts from the nearby monitoring station. Increased density at the site may foster more desirable downtown locations for businesses, offices, and residential uses over the moderate to long term.

5.7 COORDINATION AND PERMITS

Under any of the alternatives, work that disturbs 1 acre or greater ground disturbance must have a SWPPP developed and NPDES permit from the IDNR. Sediment and erosion control BMPs must be implemented. Any work located in the floodplain will need to be coordinated with the local floodplain administrator and must comply with local floodplain regulations. Cedar Rapids will issue any required building and demolition permits to its selected contractors who will be required to abide by any associated conditions according to the City's standard processes.

If contamination in excess of reporting requirements is met, work must stop, the site must be stabilized, and the IDNR must be contacted at Field Office #1 (563-927-2640). Work within the sensitive area cannot resume until IDNR clean-up or containment requirements are met and IDNR personnel indicate that no further assessment is needed at the site of the discovery. Cedar Rapids must ensure compliance with all Federal, State, and local laws regarding proper removal and disposal of asbestos containing materials and lead paint.

In the event that any archaeological deposits (soils, features, or any other remnants of human activity) are uncovered during the undertaking, this project shall be halted, the Applicant shall stop all work immediately in the vicinity of the discovery and take reasonable measures to avoid or minimize harm to the finds. The Applicant will inform IHSEMD immediately, will secure all archaeological findings and restrict access to the area. IHSEMD shall notify FEMA and FEMA will consult with the SHPO and the State Archaeologist of Iowa. Work in sensitive areas may not resume until consultations are completed or until an archaeologist who meets the Secretary of the Interior's Professional Qualification Standards determines the extent and historical significance of the discovery. Work may not resume at or around the delineated archaeological deposit until the Applicant is notified by IHSEMD.

6. CONCLUSION

The draft EA evaluated potentially significant resources that could be affected by the construction of the proposed Cedar Rapids Convention Complex Parkade. The evaluation resulted in identification of no unmitigated significant impacts associated with the resources of climate; historic; cultural; geology and soils; floodplains; wetlands and water resources; biological resources; and environmental justice. Obtaining and implementing permit requirements along with appropriate Best Management Practices and mitigation measures will avoid or minimize any effects associated with the two Alternatives considered in this EA to below the level of a significant impact. Should no significant impacts be identified during the public comment period, it is recommended that a Finding of No Significant Impact (FONSI) to the human or natural environment be issued for the Proposed Action Alternative.

7. PARTIES CONSULTED AND REFERENCES

7.1 PARTIES CONSULTED

Douglas Jones
Review and Compliance Program Manager
State Historic Society of Iowa
600 East Locust Street
Des Moines, IA 50319-0290

7.2 REFERENCES

CDM, *City of Cedar Rapids River Corridor Recovery Plan Buildings & Facilities Master Plan, Executive Summary*, Cedar Rapids, February 2009, Available: http://www.cedar-rapids.org/city-news/flood-recovery-progress/floodrecoveryplans/Pages/default.aspx, Retrieved January 13, 2012 (CDM 2009)

City Data.com, *Cedar Rapids*, Iowa, 2011, Available: http://www.city-data.com/city/Cedar-Rapids-Iowa.html, Accessed January 27, 2012

City of Cedar Rapids, *Cedar Rapids Zoning Code*, [Online], Available: http://library.municode.com/HTML/16256/level1/CH32ZO.html#TOPTITLE, Accessed February 11, 2012 (Zoning Code)

City of Cedar Rapids, *Municipal Code*, 2011, Available: http://www.cedar-rapids.org/government/departments/city-clerk/Municipalcode/Pages/default.aspx (Code 2011)

City of Cedar Rapids, *City Assessor GIS: Powered by Freeance 5.4.0.3620 – TDC Group Inc.,* 2001, Available: http://crgis.cedar-rapids.org/Freeance/Client/ PublicAccess1/index.html?appconfig=City_Assessor_GIS, Accessed February 6, 2012

City of Cedar Rapids, FEMA ESF #14, and RIO, *Long-Term Community Recovery Report*, Targeted Technical Assistance, December 2008 (Cedar Rapids, 2008)

Corridor Metropolitan Planning Organization, *Connections 2040, The Corridor MPO's 2040 Long Rage Transportation Plan*, July 15, 2010 (CMPO, 2010)

Council on Environmental Quality, *Draft NEPA Guidance on Consideration of the Effects of Climate Change and Greenhouse Gas Emissions*, February 18, 2010, Available: http://ceq.hss.doe.gov/nepa/regs/Consideration_of_Effects_of_GHG_Draft_NEPA_Guidance_FINAL_0 2182010.pdf, Retrieved January 26, 2012

Freilich, Leitner & Carlsisle, *Comprehensive Plan for Cedar Rapids*, City of Cedar Rapids, Adopted May 19, 1999 (Freilich et al., 1999)

Frey, Patrice, et al, *National Trust for Historic Preservation, Building Reuse: Finding a Place on American Climate Policy Agendas*, September 2008, [Online] http://www.preservationnation.org/issues/sustainability/additional-resources/buillding_reuse.pdf Retrieved January 20, 2012

Federal Highway Administration, *Highway Construction Noise Handbook*, FHWA-HEP-06-015, DOT-VNTSC-FHWA-06-02, NTIS No. PB2006-109102, August 2006

Iowa Department of Natural Resources, 2006, *Iowa Construction Site Erosion Control Manual*

Iowa Department of Natural Resources, *Iowa DNR Facility Explorer*, August 2011, [Online] Available: https://facilityexplorer.iowadnr.gov/FacilityExplorer/SiteDetail.aspx?facID=310803477, Accessed April 25, 2012

Iowa Department of Natural Resources, *Tier 1 Guidance: Site Assessment of Leaking Underground Storage Tanks (LUST) Using Risk-Based Corrective Action (RBCA)*, Version 1.0, November 1996, [Online] Available: http://www.iowadnr.gov/portals/idnr/uploads/ust/tier1guide.pdf, Accessed March 2, 2012

Iowa Department of Natural Resources, *UST/LUST* database, 2010 [Online], Available: https://programs.iowadnr.gov/tanks/pages/advanced.aspx, Accessed April 25, 2012

Preservation Green Lab, National Trust for Historic Preservation, The Greenest Building: Quantifying the Environmental Value of Building Reuse, 2011, [Online] Available: http://www.preservationnation.org/issues/sustainability/green-lab/lca/The_Greenest_Building_lowres.pdf, Accessed February 3, 2012

Sasaki, *City of Cedar Rapids Framework Plan for Reinvestment and Revitalization*, City of Cedar Rapids, December 2008, Available: http://www.cedar-rapids.org/city-news/flood-recovery-progress/floodrecoveryplans/Pages/default.aspx, Retrieved January 13, 2012 (Sasaki 2008)

Sasaki, *City of Cedar Rapids Neighborhood Planning Process Executive Summary*, City of Cedar Rapids, September 2009, Available: http://www.cedar-rapids.org/city-news/flood-recovery-progress/floodrecoveryplans/Pages/default.aspx, Retrieved January 13, 2012 (Sasaki 2009)

Terracon Consultants, Inc., *Limited Site Investigation,* Terracon Project No. 06117110; February 17, 2012 (Terracon, 2012)

U.S. Census Bureau, American FactFinder Website, *2010 Decennial Census*, Available: http://factfinder2.census.gov/faces/nav/jsf/pages/index.xhtml, Retrieved May 1, 2012

U.S. Environmental Protection Agency, Facility Registry System, February 17, 2011, [Online] Available: http://www.epa.gov/enviro/html/fii/, Accessed February 25, 2012

U.S. Environmental Protection Agency, *Greenhouse Gas Reporting Program: Overview*. October 5, 2009, Available: http://www.epa.gov/climatechange/emissions/downloads/FinalMRROverview.pdf, Retrieved January 26, 2012 (USEPA ,2009)

U.S. Environmental Protection Agency, *Information on Levels of Environmental Noise Requisite to Protect Public Health and Welfare with an Adequate Margin of Safety,* March 1974, Available: http://www.nonoise.org/library/levels74/levels74.htm (USEPA, 1974)

U.S. Environmental Protection Agency, *National Ambient Air Quality Standards*, 2011, Available: http://www.epa.gov/air/criteria.html (USEPA, 2011a)

U.S. Environmental Protection Agency, *Map of Radon Zones*, 2011, Available: http://www.epa.gov/radon/zonemap.html (USEPA, 2011b)

U.S. Environmental Protection Agency, *Currently Designated Non-Attainment Areas for Criteria Pollutants*, Green Book, February 14, 2012, Available: http://epa.gov/oaqps001/greenbk/ancl.html, Accessed February 23, 2012 (USEPA, 2011c)

U.S. Global Change Research Program, *Global Climate Change Impacts in the United States*, Cambridge University Press, 2009, Available: http://www.globalchange.gov/what-we-do/assessment/previous-assessments/global-climate-change-impacts-in-the-us-2009, Retrieved December 13, 2011 (USGCRP, 2009)

U.S. Fish and Wildlife Services. *Iowa Protected Species and Habitats.*

U.S. Government. 1972. *Noise Control Act, Public Law 92-574.*

U.S. Government. 1977. *Clean Water Act.*

U.S. Government. 1981. *Farmland Protection Policy Act, Public Law 98-98.*

U.S. Government. 1994. *Federal Actions to Address Environmental Justice in Minority Populations and Low-Income Populations. Executive Order 12898.*

U.S. Government. 1977. *Floodplain Management. Executive Order 11988*

U.S. Government. 2008. *Code of Federal Regulations, Floodplain Management and Protection of Wetlands Title 44, Part 9,* October 1.

U.S. Government. 1979. *Code of Federal Regulations, Housing and Urban Development Environmental Criteria and Standards, Title 24 Part 51.*

U.S. Government. 2008. *Code of Federal Regulations, Stafford Act, Title 44, Part 10,* October 1.

U.S. Government. 2008. *Code of Federal Regulations, National Environmental Policy Act, Title 40, Parts 1500-1508.* October 1.

U.S. Government. 2008. *Code of Federal Regulations, National Register of Historic Places, Title 36, Part 60.4.* October 1.

U.S. Government. 2008. *Code of Federal Regulations, National Historic Preservation Act, Title 36, Part 800.* October 1

8. LIST OF PREPARERS

8.1 GOVERNMENT PREPARERS

Eric Wieland, EHP Branch Director, Iowa Closeout Center, Federal Emergency Management Agency, Region VII

John Dawson, Environmental Protection Specialist, Iowa Closeout Center, Federal Emergency Management Agency, Region VII

Alex Cole-Corde, Environmental Protection Specialist, Iowa Closeout Center, Federal Emergency Management Agency, Region VII

Teri Toye, Historic Preservation Specialist, Iowa Closeout Center, Federal Emergency Management Agency, Region VII

Appendix A

Figure 1: General Location of Cedar Rapids Convention Complex Parkade

Source: Iowa State University Geographic Information Systems Support and Research Facility, Iowa Geographic Map Server, Summer 2011 Orthophotos – USDA (natural color), 1999-2012, Online; http://ortho.gis.iastate.edu/, Retrieved April 24, 2012

Figure 2: Historic Flood Insurance Rate Map – Cedar Rapids Convention Complex Parkade

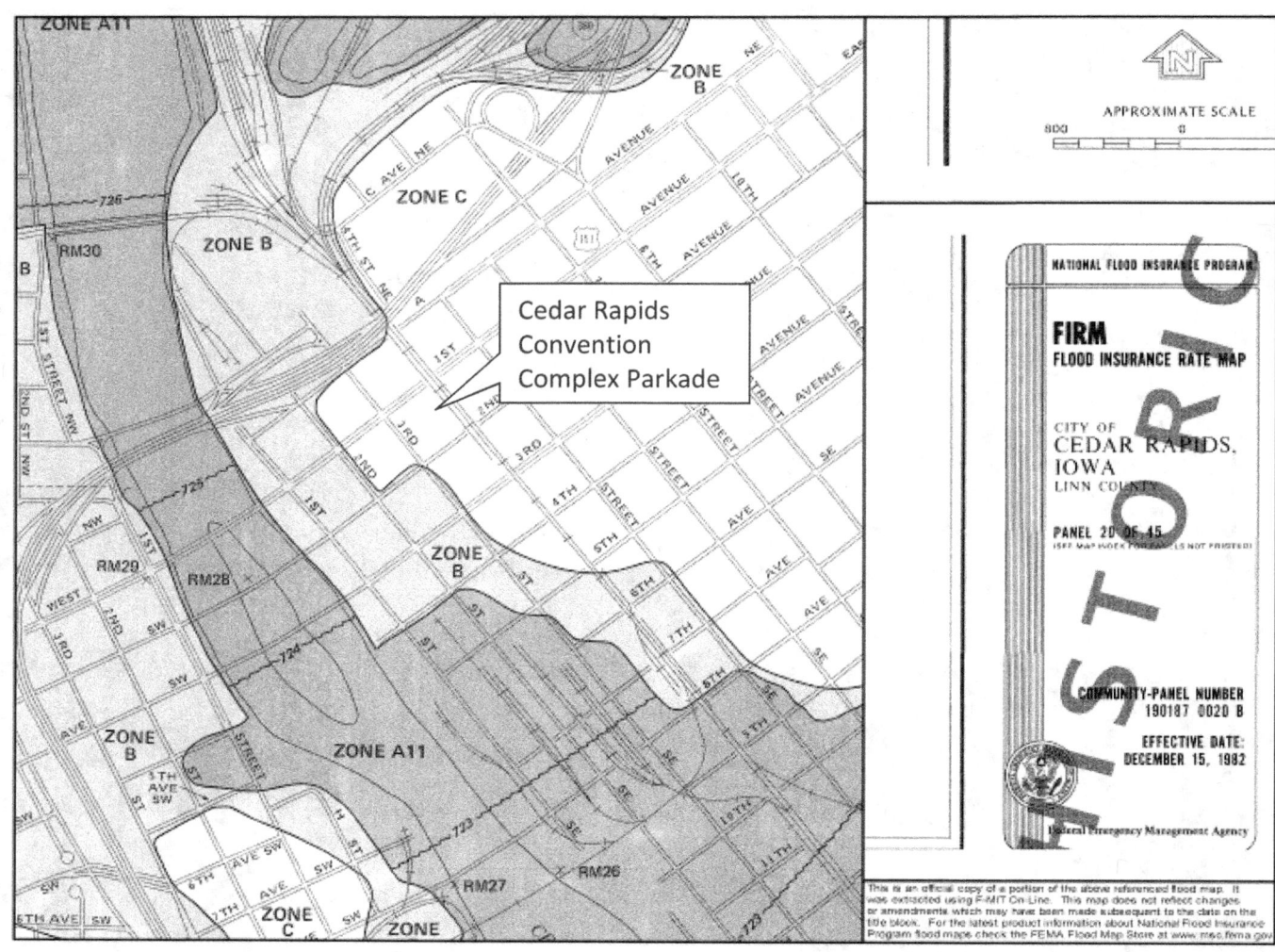

Figure 3: Current Flood Insurance Rate Map – Cedar Rapids Convention Complex Parkade

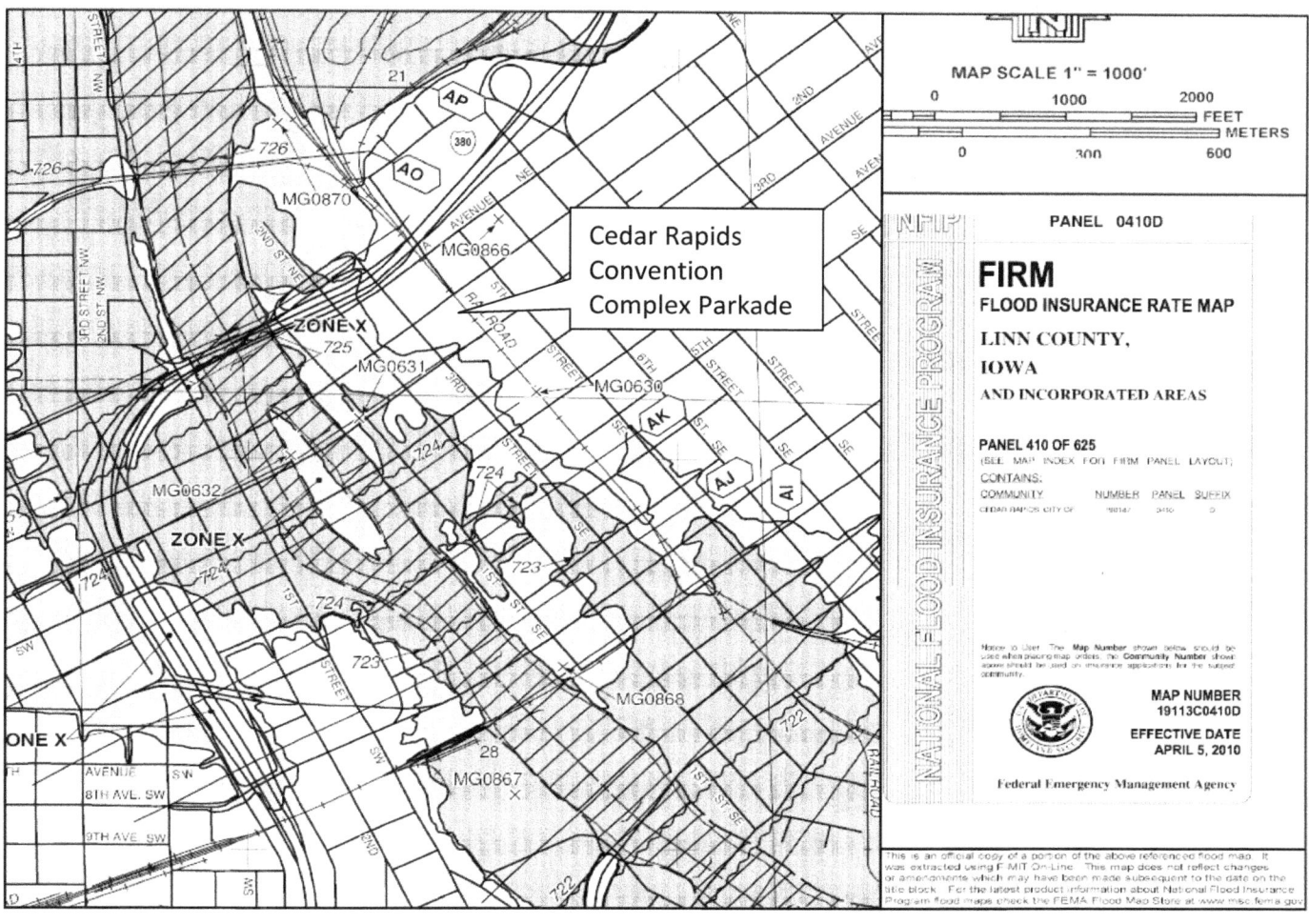

Figure 4: 2010 Census Tract Boundaries - Cedar Rapids Convention Complex Parkade

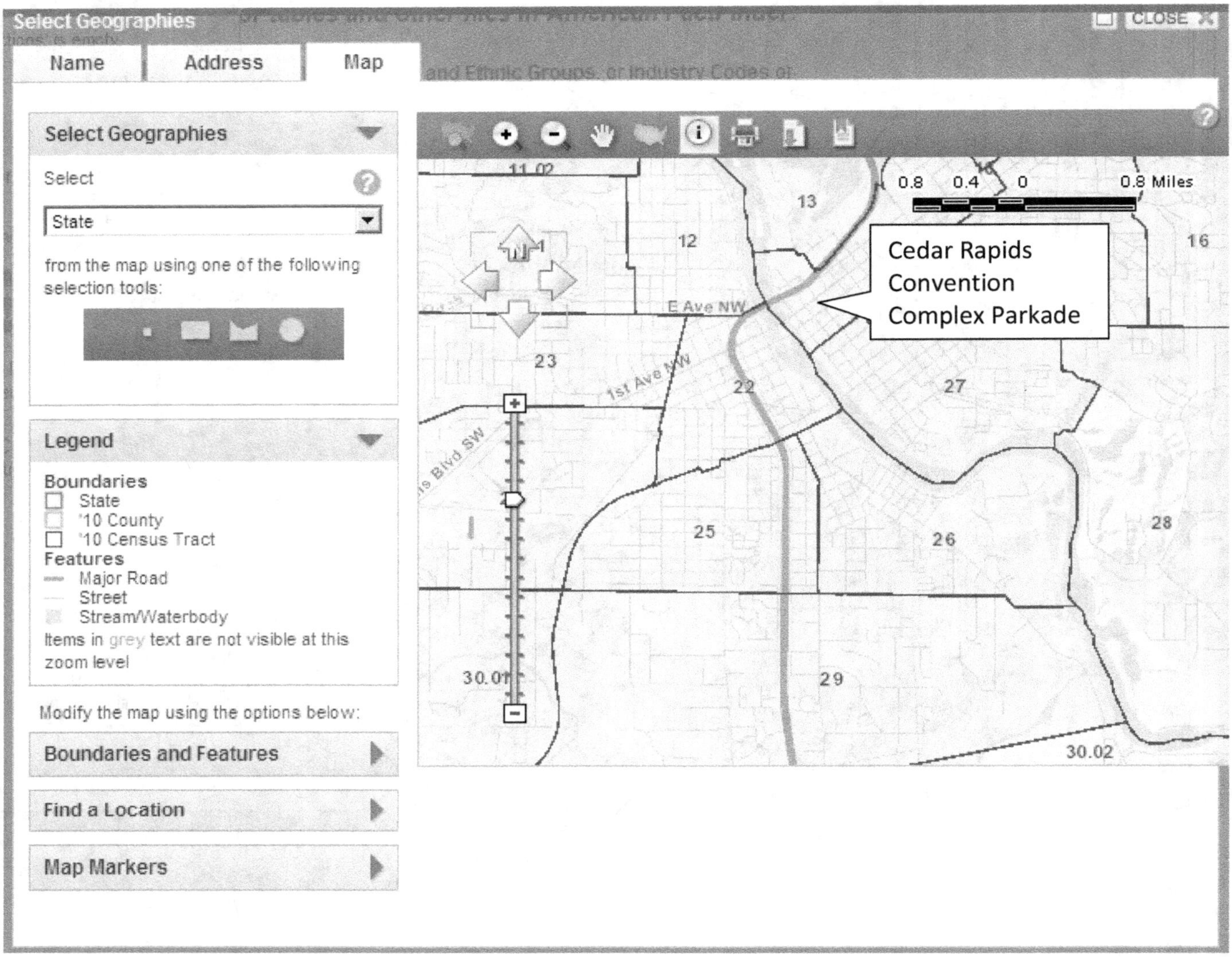

Source: American FactFinder, U.S. Census Bureau

Figure 5: Select Demographic Data - Cedar Rapids Convention Complex Parkade

	Census Tract 19	Cedar Rapids
2010 Housing Units	993	57,217
2010 Population	2,891	126,326
2010 Minority Population	485	15,182
2010 Minority Proportion	16.8%	12.0%
2010 Population reporting as Hispanic/Latino	182	4,176
2010 Proportion reporting as Hispanic/Latino	6.2%	3.3%
2010 Population by Age: Under 18	285	29,646
2010 Population by Age: Proportion under 18	9.8%	23%
2010 Population by Age: 18-64	2388	80,108
2010 Population by Age: Proportion 18-64	82.6%	63%
2010 Population by Age: Over 64	218	16,572
2010 Population by Age: Proportion over 64	7.6%	13%
2010 Median Age: Male	26.7	34
2010 Median Age: Female	22.3	36.8
2000: Median Household Income	$50,781	$43,704
2010 ACS: Poverty Percentage	35%	12.0%
2010 ACS: Poverty Margin of Error	± 9.6%	± 1%

Source: American FactFinder, U.S. Census Bureau

This EA uses data from both the 2000 and 2010 Decennial Censuses as not all data for 2010 has been released as of the writing of this EA. The American Community Survey (ACS) is also used for rough comparison as the data is more current however the data uses smaller sample sizes and has higher margins of error than the data used in the decennial censuses. As the 2008 flood heavily impacted all four Census Tracts in this EA; the 2010 Census address canvassing operation began in March 2009; and as housing acquisition funded through FEMA and Community Development Block Grants (CDBG) have been in progress since before the Census process began, the demographics of this area should be understood as dynamic and may vary from the 2010 Census data as released. Due to the sample size and the methodology used by the ACS, the real levels of population considered in poverty could vary considerably. The estimated proportion of the population of Cedar Rapids determined to be in poverty has increased with a much narrower margin of error due to the significantly larger sample size.

Figure 6: Cedar Rapids Zoning Map Excerpt – Cedar Rapids Convention Complex Parkade

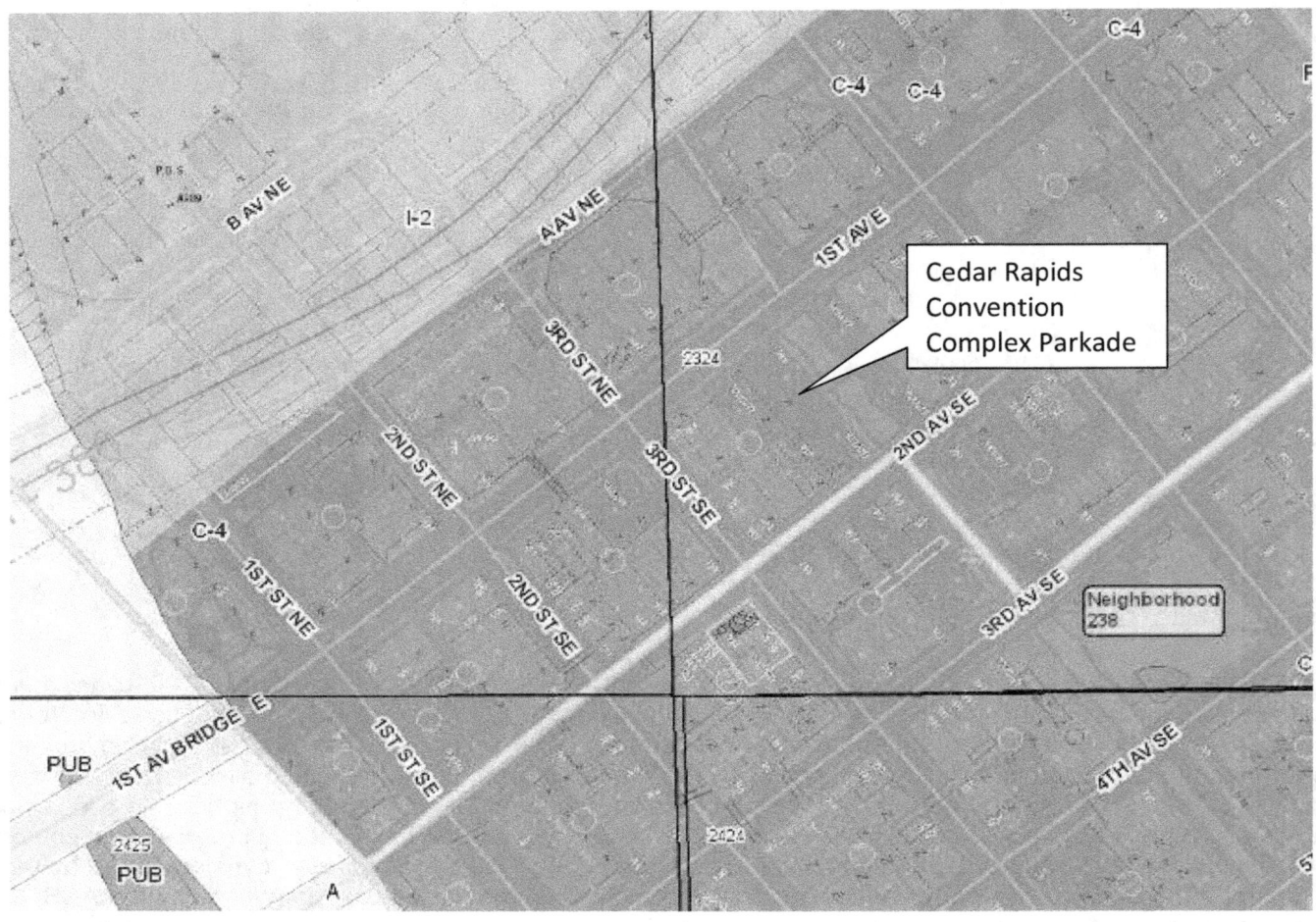

Source: Cedar Rapids Assessor GIS, Zoning Overlay: http://crgis.cedar-rapids.org/Freeance/Client/PublicAccess1/index.html?appconfig=City_Assessor_GIS.

Note: A summary of the zoning designations applicable to Figures 10-11 can be found in the City's Zoning Ordinance Chapter 32.03 available online at:
http://library.municode.com/HTML/16256/level1/CH32ZO.html#TOPTITLE.

Appendix B

Photograph #1: View across 2nd Avenue of buildings facing on the road.

Photograph #2: View across 2nd Avenue showing existing entrance of Lot 24/26.

Photograph #3: View from intersection of 2nd Avenue and Cedar River Corridor Trail of the existing surface lot.

Photograph #4: View from intersection of 2nd Avenue and Cedar River Corridor Trail of railroad adjacent to the Trail, northeast of the proposed project site.

Photograph #5: View from intersection of 2nd Avenue and Cedar River Corridor Trail along 2nd Avenue, northeast of the proposed project site.

Photograph #6: View from intersection of 2nd Avenue and Cedar River Corridor Trail along 2nd Avenue, southwest along the proposed project site.

Photograph #7: View from intersection of 2nd Avenue and Cedar River Corridor Trail to the east showing the parking lot for the Cedar Rapids Museum of Art.

Photograph #8: View of alley through proposed project site to be built over from the Cedar River Corridor Trail.

Photograph #9: View from Cedar River Corridor Trail at approximately the mid-point of the parcel showing construction of the Cedar Rapids Convention Center across 1st Avenue from the propose project site.

Photograph #10: View from the intersection of 1st Avenue and the Cedar River Corridor Trail of the project site south from the Convention Center parcel.

Photograph #11: View from the intersection of 1st Avenue and the Cedar River Corridor Trail southwest along 1st Avenue showing construction activities on the Cedar Rapids Convention Center.

Appendix C

Figure 1: First Level Schematic of Parkade

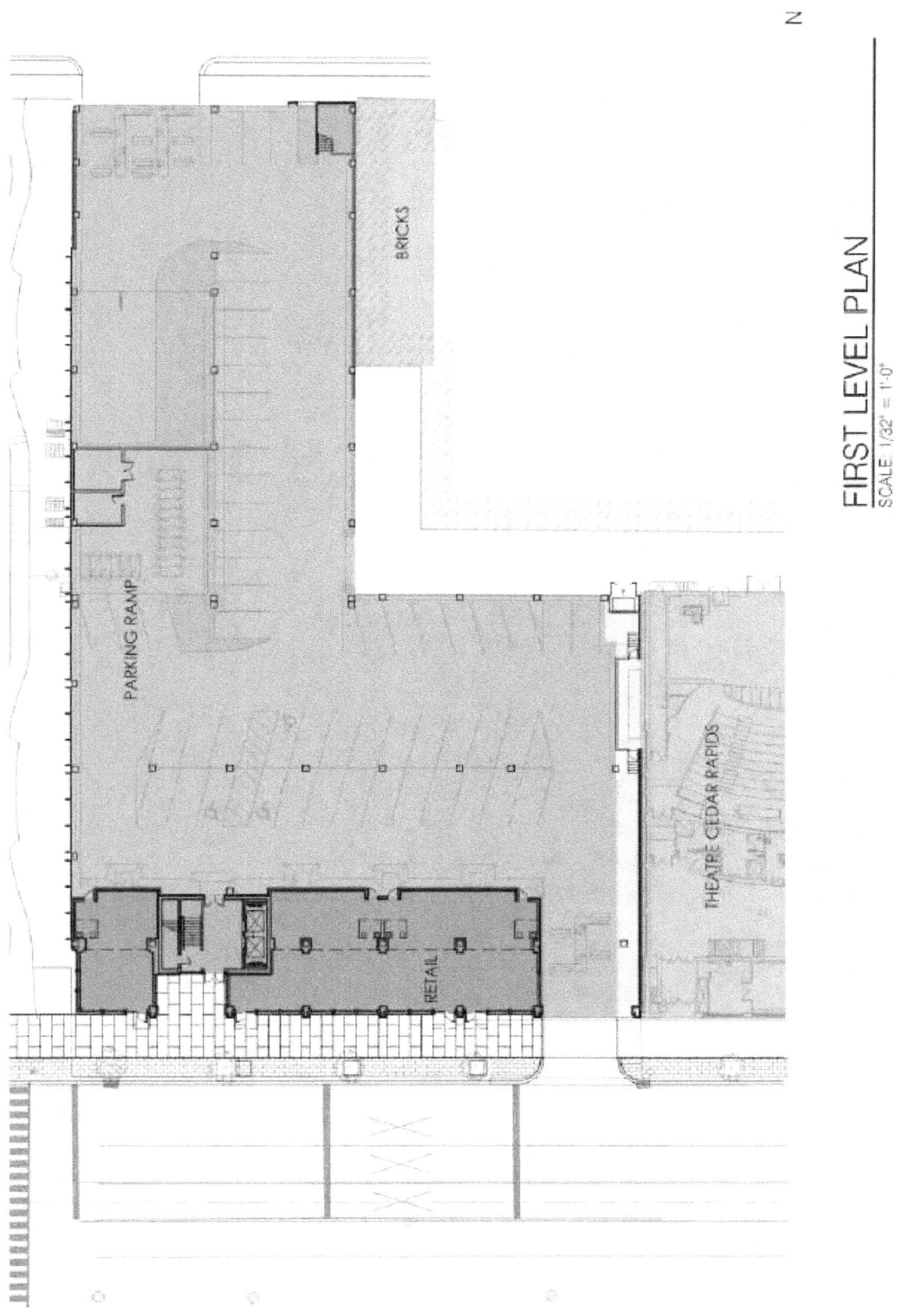

Figure 2: First Level Plan

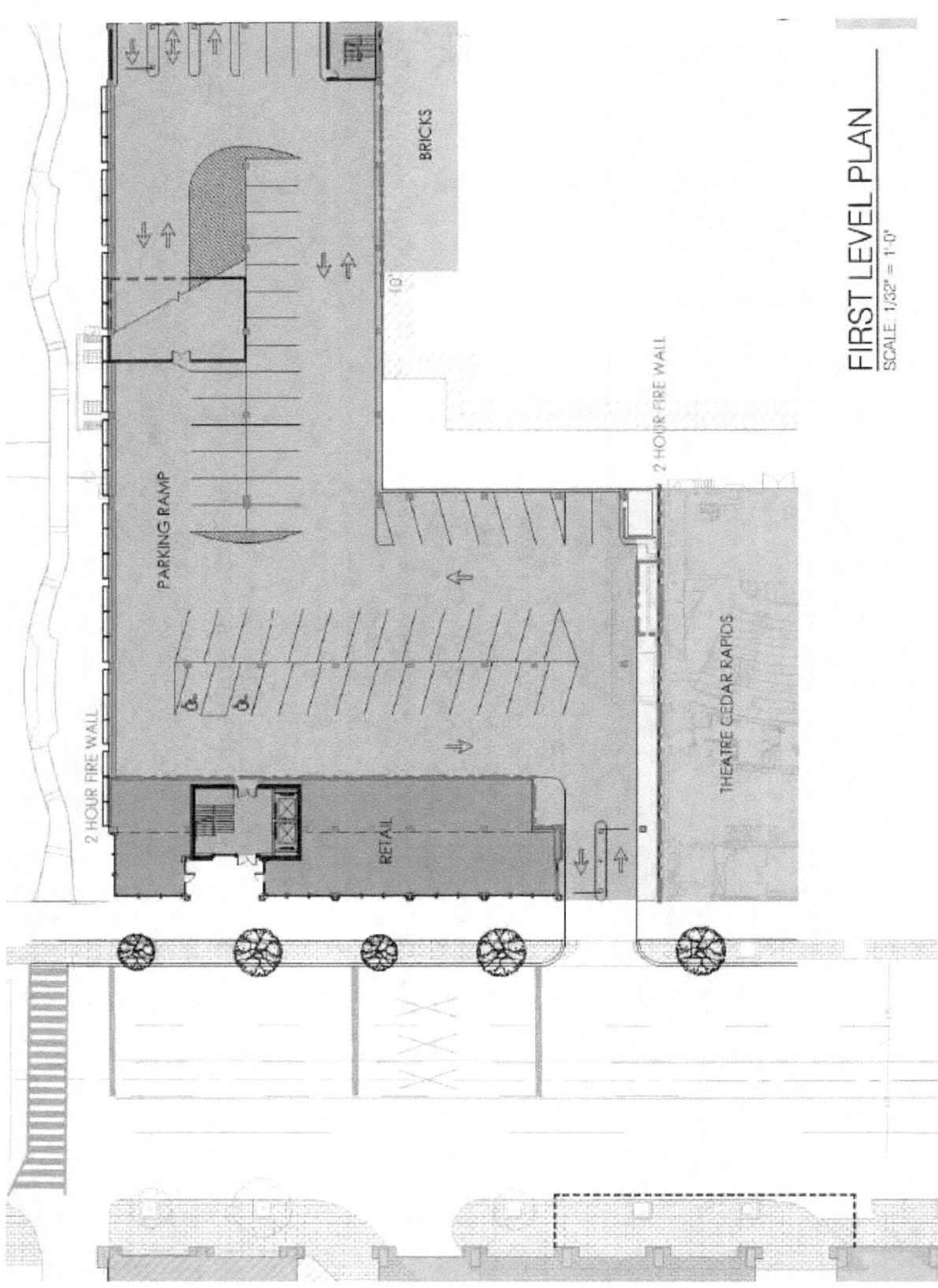

FIRST LEVEL PLAN
SCALE: 1/32" = 1'-0"

Figure 3: Third Level Plan with Skywalk

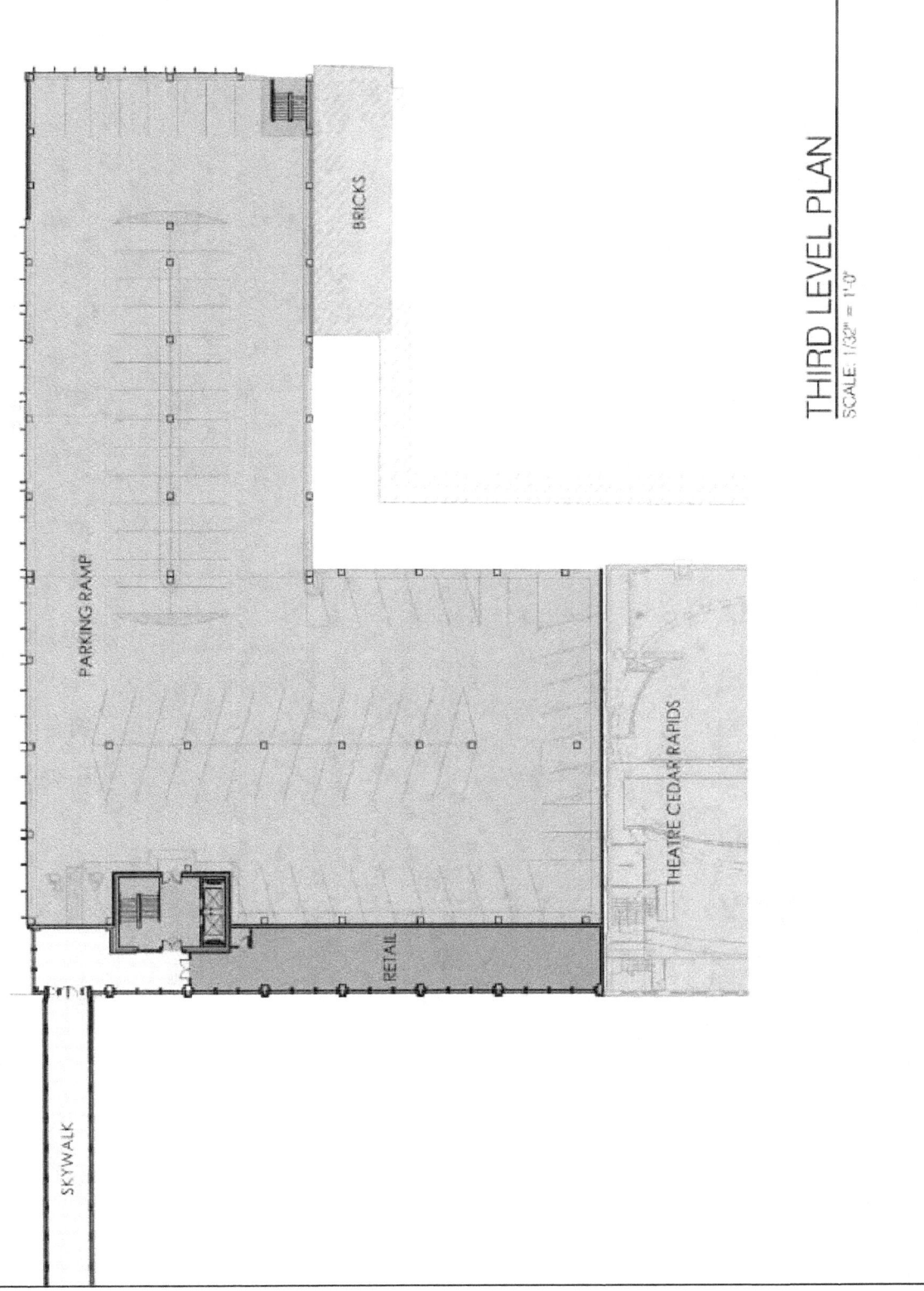

THIRD LEVEL PLAN
SCALE: 1/32" = 1'-0"

Figure 4: Top Level Plan with Roof-top Plaza

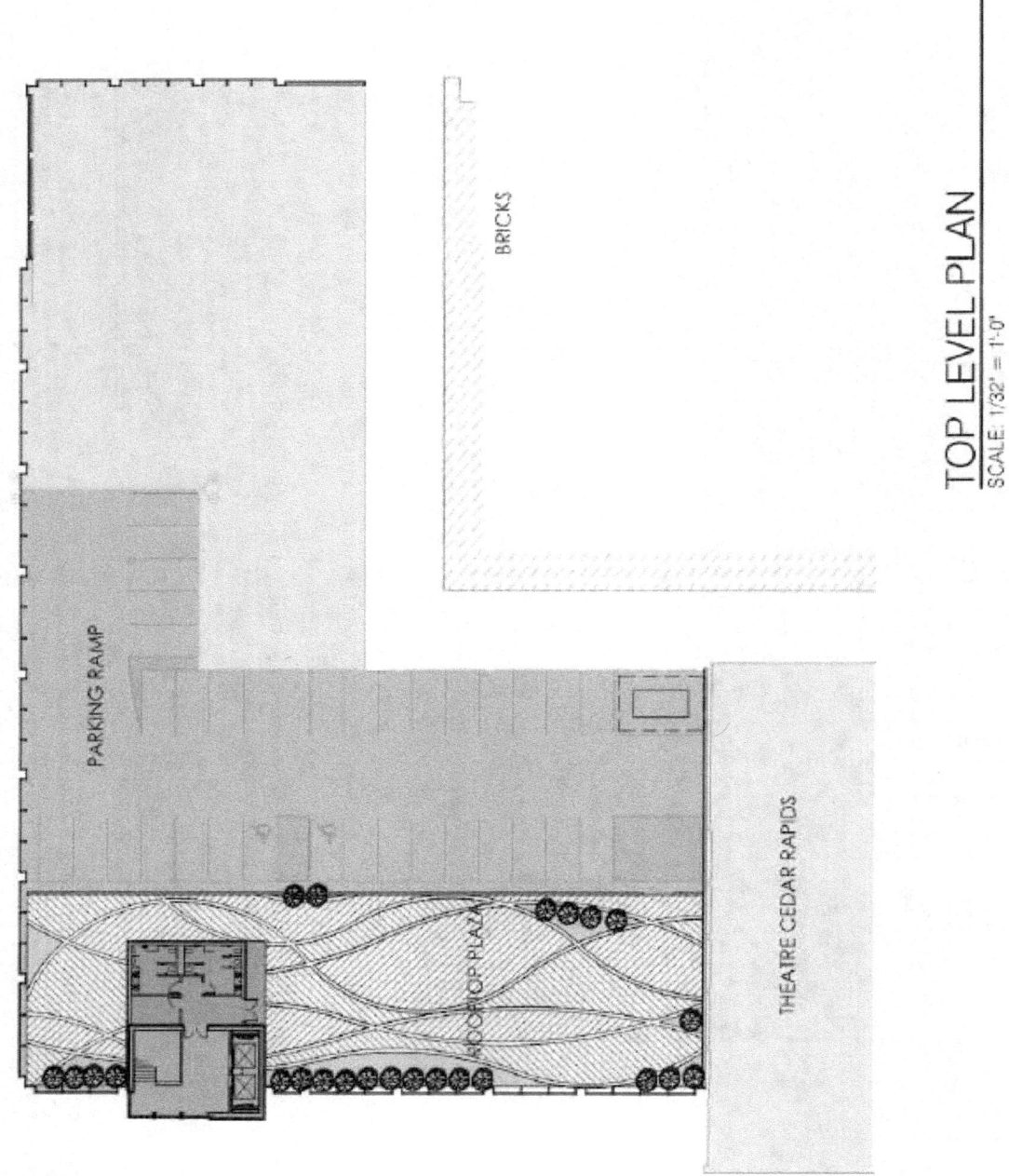

TOP LEVEL PLAN
SCALE: 1/32" = 1'-0"

Figure 5: First Avenue Elevation Rendering

Figure 6: Elevation Rendering Across Cedar River Trail and Railroad

Figure 7: Second Avenue Elevation Rendering

Figure 8: Rendering of Parkade from Intersection of Cedar River Trail and 1st Avenue

Figure 9: Rendering of Parkade from Intersection of Cedar River Trail and 2nd Avenue

Appendix D

Figure 1: NRHP Listed and Potentially Eligible Properties Excerpted from Past Survey Report

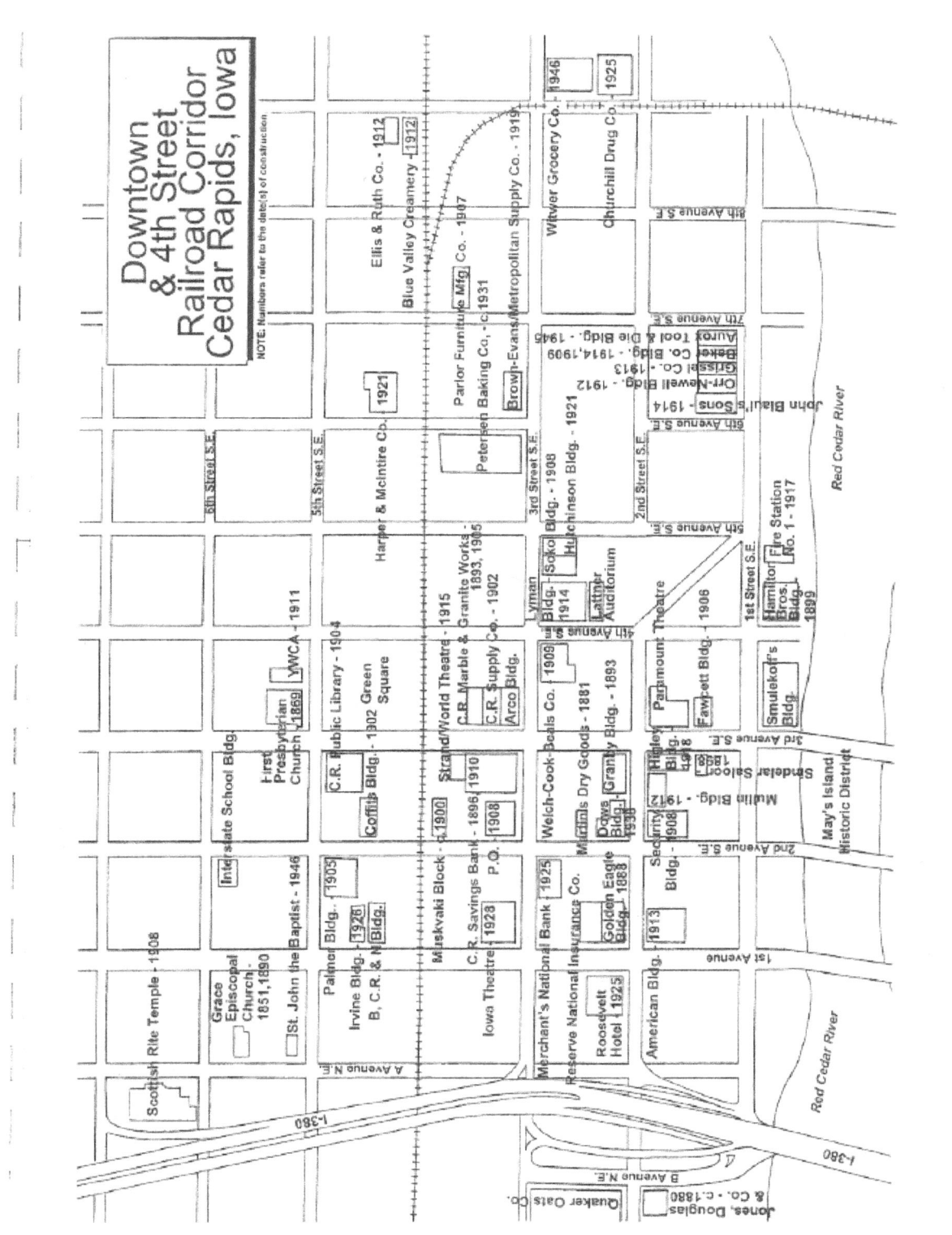

Appendix I: Potential National Register Eligible Properties

Individiual buildings and structures located throughout Cedar Rapids are associated with the commercial and industrial development of the city. The following list of properties includes buildings and sites in the downtown, along several blocks of 3rd Street, SW, in the Bohemian business district along 3rd Street, SE and 14th Avenue, SE, and along sections of several railroad corridors that crisscross the older sections of the city. Properties that have been identified include the following:[27]

<u>Downtown</u>

1st Avenue

200 1st Avenue, NE - Roosevelt Hotel, 1925 - *NRHP*
203 1st Avenue, SE - Golden Eagle Building, 1888
205 1st Avenue, SE - Reserve National Insurance Co.
301 1st Avenue, SE - Iowa Theater Building, 1928
411 1st Avenue, SE - Burlington, Cedar Rapids & Northern Building, (First Avenue Building)
417 1st Avenue, SE - Irvine Building, 1926

2nd Avenue, SE

201-207 2nd Avenue, SE - Dows Building, 1930
215-221 2nd Avenue, SE - Martin Dry Goods Co. (Ginsberg Jewelry), c. 1881
222 2nd Avenue, SE - Merchant's National Bank Building, 1925
305 2nd Avenue, SE - Cedar Rapids Post Office, (Witwer Senior Center), 1908-1910 - *NRHP*
320 2nd Avenue, SE - (Kurtz Pub)
325-329 2nd Avenue, SE -Muskvaki Block (Dragon Restaurant), c. 1900
419 2nd Avenue, SE - Coffits Building, (Hall Bicycle), 1902
526 2nd Avenue, SE - Inter-State School Building, 1908

3rd Avenue, SE

97 3rd Avenue, SE - Smulekoff's Furniture
116 3rd Avenue, SE - Sindelar Saloon, 1898
119 3rd Avenue, SE - Fawcett Building, 1906
123 3rd Avenue, SE - Paramount Theater Building, 1927 - *NRHP*
200 3rd Avenue, SE - Granby Building, 1893
302-308 3rd Avenue, SE (also 216-224 3rd Street, SE) - Cedar Rapids Savings Bank, (Guaranty Bank & Trust Building), 1896, 1910
311 3rd Avenue, SE - Cedar Rapids Supply Company, 1902
314-318 3rd Avenue, SE - Strand Theater, (World Theater), 1915
313-315 3rd Avenue, SE - Cedar Rapids Marble & Granite Works (Foreman & Clark) , 1893   & 1905
420 3rd Avenue, SE - Cedar Rapids Public Library, (Cedar Rapids Museum of Art), 1904 - *NRHP*
600 3rd Avenue, SE - First Universalist Church - *NRHP*
@ 10th Street, SE - Immaculate Conception Catholic Church

---

[27]The list of eligible and potentially eligible properties includes a building's historic name, a common name in parentheses and the construction date, if known. If a building is listed in the National Register of Historic Places the description "National Register" is also included.

1st Street, SE

101 1st Street, SE - Old Post Office (Federal Building), 1932
401 1st Street, SE - Hamilton Brother's Building (Hach's Coffee & Tea Co.), 1899 - *NRHP*
427 1st Street, SE - Fire Station No. 1 (Science Station), 1917
600 1st Street, SE - John Blaul's Sons (Great Furniture Mart), 1914
610-612 1st Street, SE - Orr-Newell Building, 1912
614 1st Street, SE - Grissel Co. Building, 1913
616 1st Street, SE - Baker Paper Co. Building, c.1914
618 1st Street, SE - Baker Paper Co. Building, 1909
620 1st Street, SE - Aurox Tool & Die Building, c.1945

2nd Street, SE

103 2nd Street, SE - American Building, 1913
118 2nd Street, SE - (Ajax Balloon)
125 2nd Street, SE - United Fire & Casualty, 1933
203 2nd Street, SE - Security Building, 1908 - *NRHP*
219-223 2nd Street, SE - Mullin Building (Drake's Salad Bar & Enzler's), 1912
225 2nd Street, SE - Higley Building, 1918
230 2nd Street, SE - Granby Building, 1893

3rd Street, SE

100-112 3rd Street, SE - Iowa Theater Building (Community Theater), 1928
216-224 3rd Street, SE (also 302-308 3rd Avenue, SE) - Cedar Rapids Savings Bank, (Guaranty Bank & Trust
                Building), 1896, 1910
302-308 3rd Street, SE -
321 3rd Street, SE - Welch Cook Beals Co. (MCI), 1909
417 3rd Street, SE - Sokolovna Gymnasium Building, 1908
419 3rd Street, SE - Hutchinson Building (Borden Building), 1921

Miscellaneous

130 B Avenue, NE - Jones, Douglas & Co. cracker factory (Ohsman & Sons Co.), c. 1880
501 A Avenue, NE - St. John the Baptist Greek Orthodox Church, 1946
525 A Avenue, NE - Grace Episcopal Church, 1851, 1873, 1890
616 A Avenue, NE - Scottish Rite Temple, 1908
217 4th Avenue, SE - Lattner Auditorium Building - *NRHP*
221 4th Avenue, SE - Lyman Building (Iowa Building), 1914 - *NRHP*
117-123 5th Street, SE - Palmer Building (MCI), 1905
310 5th Street, SE - First Presbyterian Church, 1869
318 5th Street, SE - YWCA, 1911
May's Island Historic District - *NRHP*

<u>*3rd Avenue, SW*</u>

101 3rd Avenue, SW - People's Savings Bank, (Norwest Bank) - *NRHP*
102-104 3rd Avenue SW - Gatto Building, 1912
108 3rd Avenue SW - Colonial Theater (Lederman Bail Bonds), 1914
110 3rd Avenue SW - Local Drug Co. (Stalker Electric), 1932
201 3rd Avenue SW - Acme Greeting Card Co. (Acme Graphics Building), 1924
219-221 3rd Avenue SW - Warner Building, 1911
220 3rd Avenue SW - Great A & P Tea Co. (Barron Motor Co.), 1942

Scattered Industrial Sites

Northeast Quadrant

620 17th Street, NE - Vetter & Parks Lumber Co.
200 B Avenue, NE - Quaker Oats (complex property with significant changes requiring an integrity decision based on an intensive survey of the property at a later date)
761 J. Avenue, NE - Cedar Rapids Water Purification Plant, 1930

Northwest Quadrant

805 B Avenue, NW - Dearborn Brass Foundry, (Jensen-Klich Supply Co.), 1901
807 A Avenue, NW, 707-711 B Avenue, NW & 200 8th St., NW - Chandler Pump Company, c. 1890
625 C Avenue, NW - Universal Crusher Co. (Universal Engineering Co.), 1924
605 G Avenue, NW - Cedar Rapids Pump Co., (Cedar Rapids School District Warehouse), c.1890

Southeast Quadrant

221 4th Avenue, SE - Lyman Building (Iowa Building), 1914 - _NRHP_
308 6th Avenue, SE - Petersen Baking Co. (Norand), c.1931
411 6th Avenue, SE - Harper & McIntire Co. (Smulekoff's Warehouse), 1921
317 7th Avenue, SE - Parlor Furniture Manufacturing Co., (Voelkers), 1907
402 9th Avenue, SE - Blue Valley Creamery (Cedar Rapids Sheet Metal Co.), c.1912
406 9th Avenue, SE - Ellis & Roth Co. (Cedar Rapids Sheet Metal Co.), 1912
329 10th Avenue, SE - J.G. Cherry Co., 1919
600 3rd Street, SE - Brown-Evans Manufacturing Co. (Metropolitan Supply), 1919
401 1st Street, SE - Hamilton Brother's Building (Hach's Coffee & Tea Co.), 1899 - _NRHP_
427 1st Street, SE - Fire Station No. 1 (Science Station), 1917
600 1st Street, SE - John Blaul's Sons (Great Furniture Mart), 1914
610-612 1st Street, SE - Orr-Newell Building, 1912
614 1st Street, SE - Grissel Co. Building, 1913
616 1st Street, SE - Baker Paper Co. Building, c.1914
618 1st Street, SE - Baker Paper Co. Building, 1909
900 2nd Street, SE - Churchill Drug Co./McKesson &-Robbins Co., (Hawkeye Seed Co.), 1925
321 3rd Street, SE -Welch-Cook-Beals Co., 1914
900 3rd Street, SE - Witwer Grocery Co., 1946
3rd Street, SE & 16th Avenue, SE - Sinclair and Co.-Wilson Co. site, includes nearly 100 separate but interconnected buildings: for example, Cooperage Building (Bldg.#1) dates to 1882 with others through 1970s; complex property with significant changes requiring an integrity decision based on an intensive survey of the property at a later date.

Southwest Quadrant

1115 C Street, SW - Hose Station No. 5, 1909
42 7th Avenue, SW - Iowa Pipe & Supply Co.
1201 6th Street, SW-Link-Belt Speeder Corporation, 1948, 1953, 1956, 1957
519 H St., SW - Cedar Rapids Candy Co., (Knutson Metal Co.)
1400 block Rockford Rd, SW - Rockford Road Station, CRANDIC Line

Bohemia Business District:

1326 2nd Street, SE - P. Hach Building (1901)

1006 3rd Street, SE - Suchy Building (Ryder's Saloon), 1907
1010 3rd Street, SE - (White Elephant Antiques), c. 1900

1029 3rd Street, SE - Matyk Building, 1895
1105 3rd Street, SE - C.S.P.S. Hall (Service Press), 1890, 1900, 1908 - *NRHP*
1111 3rd Street, SE - Hose Co. No. 4 (pre-1913)
1121 3rd Street, SE - Jacobs Building (1912)
1125 3rd Street, SE - Kreji Building (1911)
1129-31 3rd Street, SE - Iowa State Savings Bank, 1906
1200 3rd Street, SE - Z.C.B.J. Building (Left Bank), 1908
1201 3rd Street, SE - Iowa State Savings Bank (First Trust & Savings Bank), 1917
1317 3rd Street, SE - Lesinger Block (Little Bohemia), 1882
1318 3rd Street, SE - Zitek's Skelly Station (c. 1940)

119 14th Avenue, SE - Krejci Blacksmith, 1899
121 14th Avenue, SE - Darragh & Loufek Building, 1917
123-125 14th Avenue, SE - Karban Building, c. 1905
131 14th Avenue, SE/1401 2nd Street, SE - Martinek Hardware, c 1905
213-215 14th Avenue, SE - Ideal Theater, 1914
219-221 14th Avenue, SE - Pugh & Kucera Building, 1898
227 14th Avenue, SE and 1401 3rd Street, SE - Friendly Service Station, c. 1940

Historical and Architectural Reconnaissance Survey Report for the Downtown and Industrial Corridors in Cedar Rapids, Iowa for the City of Cedar Rapids Department of Development and the Cedar Rapids Historic Preservation Commission, April, 1997, Marlys, A. Svendsen, Svendsen, Tyler, Inc., Sarona, Wisconsin

U.S. Department of Homeland Security
9221 Ward Parkway, Suite 300
Kansas City, Missouri, 64114-3372

PUBLIC NOTICE OF AVAILIBILITY
CITY OF CEDAR RAPIDS CONVENTION COMPLEX PARKADE ENVIRONMENTAL ASSESSMENT
CEDAR RAPIDS, LINN COUNTY, IOWA
FEMA-1763-DR-IA

Interested parties are hereby notified that the Federal Emergency Management Agency (FEMA) is proposing to fund the City of Cedar Rapids' request for an improved project to construct a seven story parking structure in Cedar Rapids, Iowa under the authority of the Robert T. Stafford Disaster Relief and Emergency Assistance Act, 42 USC 5121-5207, as amended (Stafford Act, Public Law 93-288). FEMA was authorized under a Presidential disaster declaration (FEMA-1763-DR-IA) to provide Federal disaster assistance to Linn County, Iowa, as a result of the devastating flood that impacted the City of Cedar Rapids, Linn County, Iowa, beginning on June 11th, 2008.

Per the National Environmental Policy Act (42 U.S.C. 4371 *et seq.*), and associated environmental statutes, a Draft Environmental Assessment (DEA) was written to evaluate the potential impacts of the actions considered on the human and natural environment. The DEA summarizes the purpose and need, project evaluation process, affected environment, and potential environmental consequences associated with the considered options.

The City of Cedar Rapids' preferred option is to demolish the existing Lots 24/26 surface parking lot and construct a new parkade structure between 1st Avenue and 2nd Avenue with skywalk to the adjacent convention center. FEMA's Public Assistance Program has rules whereby eligible applicants may choose to use eligible, though reduced, recovery funds for improved projects. It is under these rules that the City has identified the preferred option with additional eligible funding from 280 parkway repair sites throughout downtown. The "no action" alternative, where no FEMA funds are provided for the project, is also considered in the DEA.

The public comment period will be from May 16 to June 15, 2012. Written comments on the DEA can be faxed to FEMA's Iowa Closeout Center at (515) 223-7216, emailed to Fema-ICC-EHP@fema.dhs.gov, or mailed to Environmental Planning and Historic Preservation Branch, 7755 Office Plaza Drive North, Suite 145, Building G, West Des Moines IA 50266.

The DEA can be viewed at the Cedar Rapids City Hall; at the Cedar Rapids Public Library at 221 3rd Street SE, downtown; or 2600 Edgewood Road SW at Westdale Mall; or downloaded from FEMA's website at: http://www.fema.gov/plan/ehp/envdocuments/ea-region7.shtm. If no substantive comments are received, the Draft EA will become final and this initial Public Notice will also serve as the final Public Notice.